WHY SCAMS ARE HERE TO STAY

Also by N. Ram

R. K. Narayan: The Early Years: 1906-1945 (with Susan Ram)

WHY SCAMS ARE HERE TO STAY

UNDERSTANDING POLITICAL CORRUPTION IN INDIA

N. RAM

ALEPH BOOK COMPANY
An independent publishing firm
promoted by *Rupa Publications India*

First published in India in 2017
by Aleph Book Company
7/16 Ansari Road, Daryaganj
New Delhi 110 002

Copyright © N. Ram 2017

All rights reserved.

The author has asserted his moral rights.

The views and opinions expressed in this book are the author's own and the facts are as reported by him, which have been verified to the extent possible, and the publishers are not in any way liable for the same.

No part of this publication may be reproduced, transmitted, or stored in a retrieval system, in any form or by any means, without permission in writing from Aleph Book Company.

ISBN: 978-93-84067-31-1

3 5 7 9 10 8 6 4 2

Printed at Parksons Graphics Pvt. Ltd., Mumbai

This book is sold subject to the condition that it shall not, by way of trade or otherwise, be lent, resold, hired out, or otherwise circulated without the publisher's prior consent in any form of binding or cover other than that in which it is published.

For
Wayne Barrett (1945-2017),
friend of fifty years and champion investigative reporter

CONTENTS

~

A Note on the Book   ix
Introduction   xiii

SECTION I
The Story of Corruption and Scams in India

1. Corruption and Scams as Most Indians Know Them   3
2. The Multifariousness of Corruption   15
3. Law and Enforcement   32

SECTION II
History, Definitions, and Theory

4. 'Asiatic Corruption' and the Scandal of Empire   49
5. Conceptualizing and Defining Corruption   62
6. Political Corruption Through a Marxist Lens   70

SECTION III
Two Case Studies

7. Bofors: The Defining Grand Corruption Scandal   83
8. Tamil Nadu's Scientific System of Political Corruption   106

Conclusion: What Can Be Done About	
Corruption and Scams?	133
Acknowledgements	165
Notes and References	167
Bibliography	188
Index	197

A NOTE ON THE BOOK

This book is organized into an introduction, three sections comprising eight chapters, and a conclusion.

Section I, which has three chapters, deals with the story of corruption in India—in its pervasiveness, omnipresence, and multifariousness—set against an international background. Chapter 1 discusses the phenomenon of corruption as most Indians know or perceive it. The folklore of corruption, which is itself socially important, is set against the reality of corruption and the problem of measurement is addressed. Chapter 2 highlights the diverseness of corruption. It discusses the significance and implications of the distinctions between grand corruption, petty corruption, centralized and decentralized corruption, and the issue of large-scale corruption involved in political and electoral finance. Chapter 3 deals with India's anti-corruption laws and their notoriously poor enforcement.

The second section focuses on historical, conceptual, and theoretical issues. Chapter 4 addresses the question of historical causation and culpability relating to corruption in modern India. It takes a critical look at the idea of 'Asiatic corruption' against the background of the scandal of empire. Chapter 5 engages in some detail with the challenge of conceptualizing and defining corruption. Chapter 6 is a sketch of the Marxist understanding of political corruption, which offers a radical alternative to mainstream approaches. It helps to explain, for example, why contrary to the predictions of neo-liberal economic theory, corruption has grown exponentially in the era of liberalization.

Section III comprises two case studies that speak to a much larger reality. Chapter 7 is an analysis of Bofors, India's defining grand corruption scandal. The insights and lessons presented here are drawn from my experience of leading *The Hindu*'s protracted investigation of the scandal. Chapter 8 hypothesizes that several Indian states have their own corruption systems, with well-established patterns, clear rules of the game, identifiable actors, and regional and local specificities. It draws on some original material to present a sketch of Tamil Nadu's 'scientific' system of political corruption that has been developed over the past three-and-a-half decades and has proved virtually ineradicable. This chapter proposes that focused empirical research should be conducted to build up a composite picture of the systematization of corruption arrangements across politically federal India, with implications for how to combat them.

The conclusion underlines the intractability of corruption under the prevailing circumstances, which is to say that without making deep and radical changes to India's political economy, it will not be possible to prevent and eliminate the endemic and deep-seated disorder. Subject to this general limitation, the conclusion suggests what can be done to minimize, contain, and combat corruption under nine broad heads. These proposals cover laws, enforcement capacity, policies, institutions, regulation, vigilance, the corporate sector, journalism, and politics.

N. Ram
Chennai
May 2017

INTRODUCTION

When David Davidar invited me to do a book on political corruption, drawing on my journalistic experience of investigating the Bofors scandal, for Aleph's Spotlight series, the working title he had in mind was 'India: A Corrupt Society' (with the option of having a question mark at the end). I pushed back, proposing that since corruption was a vast and unmanageable subject with too many fuzzy areas, the scope of the book should be restricted to what I thought was interesting and manageable. So this book began, as the subtitle indicates, as an attempt to get the measure of 'political corruption' in contemporary India and to see what could be done to combat it.

Political corruption is often treated as a separate and distinctive subset of corruption in journalism, in the literature of the social sciences, and by anti-corruption organizations and movements worldwide. Transparency International (TI) defines it as 'a manipulation of policies, institutions, and rules of procedure in the allocation of resources and financing by political decision-makers, who abuse their position to sustain their power, status, and wealth'[1]. But, as we shall argue in this book, this is an inadequate, indeed a blinkered view of political corruption, with serious implications for how to combat it.

As I got into the subject, delved into some of the theoretical and empirical literature, and reflected on the complex character of corruption, its sources, determinants, and effects and, crucially, the interrelationships and policy issues involved, two things became clear.

First, there is no such thing as political corruption as a self-contained category, unless you are satisfied with the tautological definition that political corruption is corruption involving politicians and political 'rents'. If the objective is to understand corruption in India in its pervasiveness, its omnipresence, and its multifariousness, so that something meaningful and effective can be done about it, necessarily in stages, it needs to be conceptualized and approached as a problem not just of politics or the economy or society, not to mention the moral sphere—but of the political economy in its complex, interdisciplinary, and profound sense.

Second, it is futile to speak of corruption at large as though it were one mode of moral and social behaviour. There is corruption and corruption and you need to disaggregate and differentiate it if you are going to get some purchase on it. This is best done by looking at the effects of specific types of corruption in society. When you do this, you can distinguish corruption that is seriously damaging from other types that are not as damaging or far less damaging or, as some political theorists suggest, even 'beneficial' in a qualified way given the circumstances (for example, by 'oiling the wheels' of a beneficial scheme, which otherwise would not get implemented at all). Making such distinctions may be hard to swallow for moral campaigners but there is simply no other way to make sense of corruption.

An explanation of the use of the word 'scam' in the title, which my publisher encouraged: scam, which has many registers and emphases of meaning but essentially denotes a swindle, is not a term that figures frequently in this book. But it is the word most widely associated with corruption in the Indian public imagination, not least because it is the word most frequently encountered in the news media. The etymology of scam is unknown but it is generally believed to be of American origin. Herman Melville's great nineteenth century novel, *The Confidence-Man*[2], set on a river boat named the *Fiddle*, is a dark and deeply ironic reflection on the act of scamming (although Melville never uses the word) as representative of 'everything that is wrong in American society in the decade preceding the outbreak of the Civil War...a time when the power of capital is transforming the American landscape, turning everything into a commodity.'[3]

Scam is not a scientific term but as a commentator on English usage points out, it 'seems to contain its meaning within the sound of the word itself—it's short and clear, and the sound is just unpleasant enough to put you on guard'[4]. It only needs to be added that Indian languages have their rich and colourful correspondences and variants for scam, again with many registers and emphases of meaning.

~

I have sometimes wondered how and why I became interested in this subject. The honest answer is happenstance: Bofors happened and found *The Hindu*, allowing us to investigate in depth, exclusively over an extended period, its well-documented secrets and offering us a rich education on the modes, devices, and dark arts of corruption at the top. If Bofors hadn't exploded in the public arena through the akratic acts of some top political leaders, senior bureaucrats, and influential businessmen, somebody may have had to invent it—but only in fiction.

Anyone seriously following Indian politics in the second half of the 1960s would have caught the scent of corruption in the air. It had not yet become the strong stench that has pervaded politics and society and proved irresistible to journalism in the twenty-first century. As a reporter starting out in the late 1960s, I was trained to be professionally sceptical of what subsequently came to be known as the folklore of corruption and the constant stream of allegations, specific as well as sweeping, made against political figures by their opponents and rivals. Not that I was particularly interested at the time in the subject of corruption. My real interest lay in reporting on issues of politics and political economy that I considered far more important, such as the political strides made by the Dravidian movement, the crisis in agrarian relations in East Thanjavur, and working-class struggles and state repression in Tamil Nadu. Yet I could not help noticing that corruption charges, which were freely traded in the political marketplace, were reported with much circumspection and, when the matter seemed to be sensitive, with awkward circumlocution in the mainstream press. 'Beware of political vendettas, verify, verify, and verify again' was the watchword in most newsrooms whenever a follow-up on a corruption allegation came up for consideration.

Since journalism was seen primarily as a discipline of verification, nobody could say this sceptical stance towards allegations made by political rivals and this obsession with fact-checking did any harm to the training and mentality of young journalists. There used to be a widely-traded joke about the verification culture at *The Hindu*: before a report or an advertisement of a natural death was published, a staff member would be dispatched to the house of the departed to make sure that he or she was not of this world. There is little doubt that over the long term the habit of verification, which is integral to the credible-information function of journalism, helps build trust in newspapers and other news media. However, as every professional journalist knows, there are areas and subjects, such as allegations of corruption levelled against prime ministers, chief ministers, ministers, and other public figures, that may not be immediately verifiable, yet are newsworthy and must be reported, analysed, and commented upon.

The press may pride itself on being a watchdog of the public interest, but it is only rarely that journalism originates a major corruption story and owns it from start to finish. Typically, it is someone off-field, a political rival, a statutory authority, an insider motivated by the call of conscience or by a less worthy or even unsavoury consideration, who blows the whistle on a major case of corruption or abuse of power[5]—and then the journalist enters the field to investigate, develop, contextualize, and present the story to the public. This is precisely what happened with the *Boston Globe*'s investigation and exposé of the pervasive sexual abuse of children by the district's Catholic clergy, a dark, yet hopeful, story brought alive with rare authenticity and emotional power by the Oscar-winning film *Spotlight*. It is Phil Saviano, a survivor of sexual abuse who heads a victims' rights group, and Mitchell Garabedian, a heroic lawyer of great humanism, who set the Spotlight team on its way to the wider truth. As though to underline the point about how a journalistic investigation begins in most cases, it turns out that the newspaper had failed to follow up very specific information on pervasive sexual abuse sent by another lawyer several years earlier.

In a long, sustained, and successful journalistic investigation of corruption, the developing story is a work in progress, usually taking the form of a series of reports culminating in a full-fledged exposé. Journalists belonging to other media organizations may also be on to the story and they may come up with new or additional information, which means that amidst competition the investigation can take on the character of a collaborative enterprise. Quite often journalists investigating major corruption face strenuous attempts at obstruction, cover-up, or worse. They need to overcome these obstacles intelligently and resourcefully before the story can be developed and presented to the public. This is the classic narrative of how investigative journalism proceeds and as a generalization it holds true for India.

However, in the late 1960s and early 1970s, any insider could see that India's criminal defamation law and other illiberal laws restricting freedom of expression were working in tandem with the conservative, play-safe norms of the newsroom to produce a dampening, if not chilling, effect on independent journalistic investigation.

Ironically, it was the Emergency of 1975-1977, with its censored and mostly supine press, that helped break the restraints. One of the unintended effects of the authoritarian Emergency, which became apparent soon after Prime Minister Indira Gandhi's Congress party was routed in the sixth general election, was the release into the arena of Indian journalism of a great deal of bottled-up investigative energy and outrage against the misuse of power and corruption[6]. The *Indian Express*'s bold and meticulously documented 1981 investigation, spearheaded by Arun Shourie, of Abdul Rehman Antulay's transgressions showed the way forward, achieving 'for the first time in recent Indian history a quest for fair name in politics—first through popular and political discourse, then through legal discourse'[7]. Other dailies and newly empowered magazines publishing in English and in various Indian languages began to take up corruption and abuse of power as a serious subject for investigation.

Around that time, as the Washington Correspondent of *The Hindu*, I too was drawn to investigative journalism. As a student at Columbia University's Graduate School of Journalism in the late 1960s, I had learnt something about a pursuit known as 'investigative reporting'. Melvin Mencher, a professor at the school, had taught us that there were different layers of reporting. As he subsequently schematized it in a textbook on news reporting and writing, Layer I reporting was 'the careful and accurate transcription of source-originated material'; digging into Layer II meant reporters initiating information-gathering and adding to Layer I material; and Layer III was 'the area of interpretation and analysis'. Investigative reporters were described as 'those who dig deepest in Layer II'. It was also possible for a skilled reporter working on a story to mine all three layers.[8]

Investigative journalism had come a long way in the decade-and-a-bit that intervened between my year at the Columbia J-School and my arrival in Washington DC as a foreign correspondent. The Watergate investigation, which was widely perceived, perhaps with some exaggeration, to have brought about the fall of President Richard Nixon, had been the game changer. Bob Woodward and Carl Bernstein, the two investigative reporters, had become household names, and journalism had become a romantic and even glamorous profession, drawing into its fold droves of young men and women who all wanted to become 'Woodsteins' so the joke went. My own ventures in investigative journalism from Washington DC had little to do with corruption or misuse of power. They had to do with investigating and making sense of the terms, and especially the conditionalities, of a five billion SDR Extended Fund Facility that had been secretly negotiated by the Indian government with the International Monetary Fund (IMF), and sensitive negotiations between the governments of India and the United States for the continued supply of low-enriched uranium fuel to operate the Tarapur Atomic Power Station.

It was only in the second half of the 1980s, after I returned to work at the newspaper's head office in Chennai, that I became intellectually and professionally interested in the subject of political corruption. A general narrative at the time, transmitted mostly in the form of rumours, went like this. The old way of raising political finance—with political workers going door to door and shop to shop to collect small sums as donations and party leaders soliciting donations from business houses—was giving way to something new and vastly different in scale. Cash donations to political parties could not be properly accounted for and sometimes raised inconvenient questions within and outside the party about the quid pro quo involved. Dealing with business lobbies and special interests that were constantly trying to call in the favours they had done to the ruling party had become something of a political nuisance.

The rulers had discovered a new, 'scientific', and apparently secure way of solving the problem: negotiate, specify, and collect a percentage of the transaction value as 'commission' on virtually every major deal signed by the government. Shell companies, offshore accounts, secret contracts, coded payments, and ways to bring the kickbacks, the dirty money, back to India had become part of an established modus operandi. A substantial part of the laundered money might have been for political and electoral funding, but given the high secrecy involved in these arrangements, the line between receiving and deploying the kickbacks for political purposes and receiving and spiriting them away for personal aggrandizement became blurred and eventually disappeared. This was the general narrative of top-level corruption doing the rounds in political and journalistic circles in the second half of the 1980s.

Then in 1987-1988, without much forewarning, we in *The Hindu* found ourselves in the deep end, investigating *grand corruption* of a kind that India had not seen before. The origins of the term, which is now widely used in international anti-corruption discourse, go back to Hegel's famous characterization of the state of the pre-Reformation Catholic Church as 'a great and general corruption' rather than an 'abuse' of a system that was intrinsically good[9]. The grand corruption in the Indian case was the great and general corruption that had come to prevail in the defence sector, which exploded in the political arena in early 1987.

The man who lit the fuse was a conscientious and somewhat unpredictable political insider, Vishwanath Pratap Singh. As Prime Minister Rajiv Gandhi's finance minister, he had won public acclaim by launching an offensive against gold smuggling, tax fraud, and the fringes of the black economy. This was politically embarrassing but hardly a threat to the Congress government, which commanded an unprecedented majority in Parliament. It was when, in an act of spectacular political miscalculation, the Prime Minister moved V. P. Singh to the Ministry of Defence that the government found itself in serious trouble. The new Defence Minister immediately busied himself with enquiring into the opaque system of defence procurement, which was rumoured to be riddled with corruption involving political leaders, senior bureaucrats, military officers, and middlemen. In April 1987, without consulting the Prime Minister who would have surely countermanded the decision, V. P. Singh ordered an investigation into suspected payoffs in the government's purchase of submarines from Howaldtswerke-Deutsche Werft (HDW). Unsurprisingly, he was forced to resign and walked away with the halo of an anti-corruption warrior. Four days later, Bofors exploded in the political arena through a broadcast by Swedish Public Radio.

Bofors is independent India's defining grand corruption scandal. This has little to do with the size of the bribes involved, ₹64 crore or $50 million (at the prevailing exchange rate), which is an insignificant proportion of the corruption involved in a major twenty-first century scandal. The various acts of corruption and, no less important, the cover-up and obstruction of justice were committed, connived at, or enabled at the highest level of government. There was manipulation and distortion of defence acquisition policies, which when exposed undermined trust in the whole system of defence acquisition. In fact, the Bofors scandal had a dampening effect on the acquisition of major weapons systems, especially heavy artillery, for the Indian armed forces. The secret payoffs into coded Swiss bank accounts were indisputably at the expense of the public good. And the central functioning of the state was badly affected by the scandal.

Bofors might have had its ups and downs, its ebb and flow in the public mind; some of the key players died during the investigation and prosecution; and the legal case eventually came to a dead end. But unlike previous and subsequent corruption scandals, this remained on the national political agenda, active and visible or lurking in the shadows, for a long time—because the political, moral, and systemic issues it raised were both deep-seated and dramatic. The distinction of Bofors was to serve over more than a decade as a metaphor for political corruption at the top. Its unravelling, in stages, in the press helped well-informed and politically conscious Indians gain a rare insight into how various institutions perform in relation to corruption.

Two Major Developments

This book on political corruption has been invested with fresh context by two recent and major developments.

The first is Prime Minister Narendra Modi's midnight shock of 8 November 2016, decreeing that primarily in order 'to break the grip of corruption and black money', the five hundred rupee and thousand rupee currency notes in use would no longer be legal tender[10]. Overnight, about 86 per cent of the total value of currency, held in these notes, was invalidated. It quickly became evident that demonetization was undertaken 'without forethought or preparation…threw the entire economy out of gear' and has taken a toll on 'an already slowing economic growth rate'[11]. It inflicted tremendous hardship, disruption, and anxiety on hundreds of millions of Indians, especially daily wage earners, other sections of the working classes, and small- and medium-sized businesses, across the country.

So what were the compensating advantages and benefits?

Demonetization was claimed to be a devastating 'surgical strike' on black money, which although not synonymous with corruption is enmeshed with it. But contrary to the stated aim, virtually all the high value notes targeted by demonetization came back into the banking system by 30 December 2016, the deadline for depositing the demonetized currency. This meant that it would be left to the income tax department, with its inadequate staff resources, to sort out the black money component from the total stock of invalidated currency deposited in banks. Under these circumstances, the probability of missing out on big black money holders, who had found ingenious ways to convert their high-denomination notes into 'white' bank deposits, was high; and the scope for harassment of the innocent and for extractive corruption seemed to have increased.

More significantly, as three recently published books on demonetization, the motivations behind it, and its effects, bring out[12], the exercise has not made a dent in India's gigantic black economy. After the surgical strike, the black economy, which Arun Kumar estimates at ₹93 lakh crore ($1.4 trillion), or 62 per cent of GDP, remains wholly intact. Nor is there any evidence that demonetization has met the other three objectives listed by the Prime Minister—combating corruption, counterfeit currency, and terrorist funding.

The Bharatiya Janata Party's (BJP) landslide victory in the 2017 Uttar Pradesh (UP) Legislative Assembly election can be interpreted to mean that demonetization did not hurt the party's electoral prospects in India's most populous state. It might even have helped to shore up the party's, and Prime Minister Modi's, political image and stock. It is also possible that as an election issue demonetization was overridden, or marginalized, by other issues and factors; the outcomes of the Assembly elections in Punjab, Goa, and Manipur, where the BJP either fared poorly or did not win as many seats as the Congress, suggest that this was probably the case. In any event, the UP electoral outcome was a sharp reminder that policies and their soundness must be viewed and evaluated quite separately from the political success or failure of those who adopt these policies.

The second major development of relevance to the fight against political corruption is the final verdict of the Supreme Court of India in the Jayalalithaa disproportionate assets case[13]. The offences under the Prevention of Corruption Act that were prosecuted, tried, and finally adjudicated in 2017 go back to the period 1991-1996, J. Jayalalithaa's first term as chief minister of Tamil Nadu. The criminal trial went on for eighteen years during which the charismatic politician was sworn in no fewer than four times as chief minister. In September 2014, the Special Court constituted to try the corruption charges and other related offences against Jayalalithaa and three others convicted and sentenced them to four years' simple imprisonment in addition to levying heavy fines. In May 2015, the High Court of Karnataka reversed the trial court's verdict, acquitting all four convicts of all the charges. Chief Minister Jayalalithaa died in December 2016 and consequently the appeals relating to her stood abated by the time the Supreme Court delivered its judgment. In February 2017, the Supreme Court set aside the judgment of the Karnataka High Court and restored in full the trial court's conviction and sentencing of the three others who were held to be active conspirators in laundering Jayalalithaa's 'ill-gotten wealth'.

Now for some counterfactual history, which asks and

attempts to answer 'what if' or counterfactual questions of some historical significance in order to gain some new insights. Had she lived, sixty-eight-year-old Jayalalithaa might have become the first chief minister to have her or his conviction and sentence for corruption offences upheld by the highest court in the land. By sending her back to prison and disqualifying her from holding office for nearly a decade, it would have effectively put an end to her political career. That would have been a landmark in the fight against high-level corruption, signalling that corrupt political leaders could no longer rely on the immunity they had enjoyed for decades at the bar of public prosecution. Unfortunately, the Supreme Court's finding that Jayalalithaa's guilt in the disproportionate assets case had been fully established in the trial came too late for its judgment to be treated as a landmark. The second best thing happened: the country was spared the prospect of another notoriously corrupt politician-in-the-making, V. K. Sasikala, who had none of Jayalalithaa's capabilities, acumen, and popular appeal but had managed to have herself installed, as Amma's successor, as party leader, being sworn in as chief minister of a major state.

Crime and punishment in Tamil Nadu is an integral part of the story of corruption in India. It bears emphasis that the case in which the guilt of a powerful, although dead, chief minister was finally upheld, and a chief ministerial aspirant was sent to prison and eight years of political banishment in 2017 by the highest court of the land goes back nearly two decades. What is clear is that the legal troubles and political setbacks that Jayalalithaa and some other political leaders, notably Lalu Prasad, Madhu Koda, Y. S. Jagan Mohan Reddy, B. S. Yeddyurappa, the Bellary brothers, and A. Raja[14], have faced over the years on account of alleged corruption have failed to act as a deterrent.

In fact, twenty-first century India has seen corruption increase exponentially at all levels—central, state, and local. In several states, corruption involving politicians, bureaucrats, businesspersons, and, in some cases, criminal elements has graduated to a new qualitative stage, transforming itself into a well-oiled, rule- and rate-bound, and self-propelled system of collecting and sharing the illicit spoils of office.

As we shall see in the following chapters, corruption today is pervasive, omnipresent, and diverse, covering every branch of the Indian state and key sectors of the economy. Everything about it suggests that it has become an intractable problem.

SECTION I

THE STORY OF CORRUPTION AND SCAMS IN INDIA

ONE

CORRUPTION AND SCAMS AS MOST INDIANS KNOW THEM

Corruption in India is almost as leaden a cliché as hunger. It is sanctified by the oldest of traditions: it is denied by nobody, indeed the totality and pervasiveness of Indian corruption is almost a matter of national pride...

—James Cameron in *Indian Summer*, 1974

Corruption in India, as the journalist James Cameron, a great friend of India, discovered, is a huge beast that everyone talks about, feels strongly about, and imagines he or she knows a lot about. Moreover, virtually everyone experiences it at some time in some form—open or hidden, flagrant or disguised, small-scale or big. In a land where myths and fantastical notions abound, it is not surprising that in the public mind this beast, which is constantly in the news, can assume fantastic forms and proportions. The 'folklore of corruption'[1] that has developed over time is itself socially and politically significant, almost on a par with the reality of the beast. It says a great deal about how millions of ordinary Indians think and feel about the high and the powerful, especially their rulers, and about the system that determines the terms of their life and work. What they do about this is another matter.

The view that corruption is pervasive and omnipresent in Indian society is not of recent origin. It goes back to the days of the East India Company. It was, in fact, shaped by its senior officials and its 'nabobs', who, returning home with huge fortunes, became a byword for the 'new corruption' in eighteenth-century Britain. East India Company officials were the major perpetrators of corruption in India but the colonial narrative made it appear that it was an endemically corrupt society that had ensnared them in its coils. In an infamous defence of his own venality, Robert Clive, the founder of British imperium in India, gave expression in 1772 to the view that it was impossible to avoid the giving and receiving of costly 'presents' in the country[2]. In a private letter written to a Tory politician, the East India Company's third Governor-General, Cornwallis, confided that he 'really' believed 'every native of Hindostan' to be corrupt[3]. Edmund Burke, political theorist and ideological champion of empire, agonized over the dangers posed to British institutions and society by the encounter between the oppression, brutality, and corruption of some of the East India Company's officials and the 'perennial spring' of Indian corruption[4]. The colonial discourse on the totality, incurability, and inescapability of 'Asiatic corruption' took powerful hold in India, colouring the way people belonging to various sections thought and felt about corruption and abuse of power in their society. It continues to exercise its influence to this day.

There have been some attempts to get the measure of corruption in independent India. The first serious attempt was the Santhanam Committee. Officially known as the Committee on Prevention of Corruption and comprising six members of parliament and a couple of officials, it was tasked by the central government in 1962 to 'review the problem of corruption and make suggestions'. It had the following to say on the challenge of definition:

> The problem of corruption is complex, having roots and ramifications in society as a whole. In its widest connotation, corruption includes improper or selfish exercise of power and influence attached to a public office or to the special position one occupies in public life. In this sense, the problem would have to be viewed in relation to the entire system of moral values and socio-economic structure of society which we could not undertake.[5]

In its report, the committee made it clear that it was primarily concerned with investigating corruption insofar as it related to the central government and its employees. However, even for this limited purpose, it needed to consider the problem in 'a somewhat wider setting'. Admitting the difficulty of defining corruption precisely, the committee cited the relevant provisions made by different laws for different purposes before settling for a working definition of 'the most common form of corruption'—a public servant securing a pecuniary or other material advantage, other than legal remuneration, directly or indirectly for himself or his family or relatives or friends. But not quite satisfied with this definition, it entered an open-ended caveat: 'other forms of the evil are coming into existence in the ever-increasing complexities of modern society'.

The committee pulled no punches in going after the supply side of corruption:

> Corruption can exist only if there is someone willing to corrupt and capable of corrupting…both this willingness and capacity to corrupt is found in a large measure in the industrial and commercial classes… The tendency to subvert integrity in the public services instead of being isolated and aberrative is growing into an organised, well-planned racket.

Gunnar Myrdal took up the subject as a theoretical problem in Chapter 20 of his monumental and analytically fertile but largely forgotten work, *Asian Drama: An Inquiry into the Poverty of Nations*.[6] He began by attributing major social significance to the folklore of corruption that he encountered in India and other South Asian countries in the 1960s. He found that the problem of corruption was 'very much on the minds of articulate South Asians', with newspapers devoting much space and political assemblies much time to it and informal conversation turning frequently to political scandals. He heard articulate voices asserting that corruption was rampant and growing, especially in high places. He noted that ostentatious efforts to prevent corruption and claims that the corrupt were being dealt with as they deserved only served to fuel cynicism, 'especially as to how far all this touches the "higher-ups".' Myrdal offered the interesting insight, from his decade-long research for *Asian Drama*, that in India and other South Asian countries the folklore of corruption, which was predominantly about corruption in high places, embodied 'important social facts' and profoundly influenced the way people conducted their lives and how they viewed the government's national consolidation and development efforts.

Among those who have subsequently written on corruption in India, attitudes towards this folklore have varied. While explaining its sources and roots, the legal scholar Upendra Baxi pleads for its minimization because it could undermine people's faith in democracy and pave the way for authoritarianism. His plea, possibly with the experience of the Emergency of 1975-1977 in mind, is: '*Minimise*, please, as far as is humanly and democratically possible, the folklore of corruption. Not *every* Indian politician is corrupt and dishonest.[7] [emphasis in original] The economist Pranab Bardhan apprehends that the widespread perception that everyone around is corrupt 'can sometimes actually increase corruption, as otherwise honest people yield to temptation more easily, since the chances of being individually detected are smaller, the expected reputation loss on detection is less important, and the search cost for finding a briber is less'[8]. Myrdal himself wondered whether the folklore reflected 'a weak sense of loyalty to organised society…a general asociality'[9], and even corruption-envy. But he veered towards the conclusion that all things considered, the public outcry against corruption was a constructive force that needed to be harnessed to support a government willing to undertake serious reform.

More recent research by the anthropologist Akhil Gupta into localized corruption, situated within a context of an uncaring and oppressive state, structural violence, and life-denying poverty, reveals that the folklore, at least in some regions of the country, is alive, in rude health, and well-informed about bhrashtaachaar (corruption in its variegated forms) and the state, with the rural poor emerging as 'knowledgeable social actors' who understand that 'learning more about the state was an invaluable aid to improving one's life chances in the world'[10]. Gupta pays special and respectful attention to the stories about corruption, noting that they usually had 'the formal properties of narratives: a central character or subject; a sequence of events that led to a change or reversal of an initial situation; and a causal explanation for the change that culminated in a revelation or lesson'. This suggests the possibility that, artistic value aside, the folklore has its nose to the ground, capturing a lot more of the reality, modes, and specifics of decentralized corruption than its critics allow.

Myrdal, who was primarily concerned with the implications of pervasive corruption for the South Asian region's political stability and national development efforts, proposed that the topic could be understood and researched as the interplay of three phenomena: first, the *folklore*, to be precise 'people's beliefs about corruption and the emotions attached to these beliefs, as disclosed in the public debate and in gossip'; second, *anti-corruption campaigns*, that is, public policy measures and legislative, administrative or judicial institutions set up to 'enforce the integrity of public officials at all levels'; and finally, the *facts* of corruption, which would include the nature, form, and extent of corruption and specifics such as the numbers of the corrupt, the positions they hold, and their modus operandi. All three phenomena were related to wider problems reaching into 'the murkier depths of social reality'[11].

Myrdal even came up with a 'sketch' of a theory of corruption in South Asia by offering some 'reasonable, though quite tentative' questions to be explored and hypotheses to be tested. These questions and hypotheses attempted to relate corruption in South Asian countries to general socio-economic conditions, to the stage of development, and especially to institutional and attitudinal problems. But Myrdal's sketch of a theory of corruption in South Asia was ahistorical in one critical respect: it failed to acknowledge the extent to which the colonial power had participated in and nurtured the corruption, and the conditions engendering corruption, that free India inherited. Interestingly, while Myrdal saw the *presence* of corruption in South Asian countries in somewhat static terms, as a legacy from pre-capitalist, traditional society, he related the *increase* in corruption to the processes of dynamic change in the social system, offering the insight that many of the changes that had occurred afforded 'greater incentives as well as greater opportunities for corruption'. Most significantly, he called attention to the active role of the business world in promoting corruption among politicians and administrators.

Socio-economically and politically, India is a very different country from the one Myrdal encountered during the decade he researched and wrote *Asian Drama*. But his observation that many of the dynamic changes in the social system had enabled corruption on a bigger scale proved prophetic for the post-1991 era of economic liberalization and accelerated pursuit of neo-liberal policies. It is now well established that the facts of corruption, that is, its magnitude, spread, and effects in the polity and society, have increased exponentially over the past quarter century. While the folklore has kept in step, the anti-corruption arrangements and actions have been limping a long way behind.

The problem in India, where moralistic approaches to corruption are common and often dominate public discourse, is that the gap between what the anti-corruption campaigners, many of them 'Gandhians', demand and what the polity and the legal system are willing and able to do is enormous. When corruption is not conceptualized soundly, in relation to socio-economic, political, and cultural factors, but is presented in overly simplified moral terms, analysis of its causes and effects tends to go all over the place; and without accurate, theoretically sound and empirically backed analysis, prescription tends to be seriously flawed. The result is that anti-corruption institutional arrangements and actions habitually miss the mark; and mass campaigns against corruption, fuelled largely by moral outrage, make their contribution by raising the level of public awareness but are unable to sustain themselves beyond a point and fail to meet the lofty objectives they set themselves. The anti-corruption movements spearheaded by Jayaprakash Narayan in the 1970s and by Anna Hazare in 2011-2012 make the case strongly for the last point.

The past decade-and-a-half has seen a spectacular outbreak of corruption scandals, big-ticket, medium-sized, and relatively small. With its tentacles spreading to virtually every branch of the Indian state, including the judiciary, and to key sectors of the economy, notably finance, construction, mining, land and real estate, information technology, telecommunications, agriculture, and defence, and to the news media, corruption's salience in India's political economy and public policy discourse has never been higher.

For the period 2000–2013, Sukhtankar and Vaishnav, researchers in political economy, have come up with a shortlist of twenty-eight scams[12], involving hundreds of billions of dollars, from the lists compiled by five news outlets. The shortlist ranges from the Cash for Votes scandal of 2008, where the alleged bribes to members of parliament aggregated a mere ₹50 crore[13], to the Commonwealth Games scam of 2010, where the embezzlement soared to ₹70,000 crore; from the Adarsh Housing Society scandal, where the value loss to the government was ₹163 crore, through the 2G Spectrum scam (₹56,000 crore) to Coalgate (₹186,000 crore) and the Antrix Devas/ISRO Spectrum Allocation (₹200,000 crore) scandals; from the Taj Heritage Corridor scam (₹175 crore) to the Uttar Pradesh National Rural Health Mission (₹10,000 crore), the Maharashtra Irrigation Scam (₹35,000 crore), and Foodgrains scandal (₹35,000 crore). The list includes two defence deal scams (Tatra Trucks and AgustaWestland Helicopters) and five mining scandals involving several states. It includes seven cases of corruption categorized by the authors as 'private fraud' and estimated to aggregate ₹101,435 crore; the notables here are the Telgi Stamp (₹43,000 crore), the Sahara India Pariwar Investor (₹24,000 crore), the Saradha Group Chit Fund (₹20,000 crore), and the Satyam Computer Services (₹14,162 crore) mega-swindles. Sukhtankar and Vaishnav calculate that for their shortlist of early twenty-first-century corruption scandals, 'the mean scam "value" was ₹36,000 crore, and the median ₹12,000 crore'.

A major omission from this shortlist is Vyapam, the mega-scam in BJP-ruled Madhya Pradesh which I discuss in Chapter 8.

There was a time when the stock explanation for corruption in India was the 'permit-licence-quota raj'—virtually everything could be attributed to it. The prediction offered by a legion of neo-liberal economists and political theorists was that deregulation and liberalization would lead to the prevention, containment, and eventual elimination of corruption. Precisely the opposite has happened: liberalization has ushered in corruption in a much greater variety of forms and on an unimaginably greater scale than anything seen under the so-called licence raj.

The interesting question is why and various answers have been put forward by scholars and policymakers. The essential neo-liberal answer is that many vestiges of the licence raj remain, enforcement capacity is still weak, and the reform process needs to be given more time to bring down the level of corruption. The evidence clearly and decisively goes against such ideologically-led reasoning that often sounds like casuistry. The real explanation for the exponential increase in corruption in the era of liberalization and high economic growth must necessarily be complex and nuanced and, as we will see in Chapter 6, it is to be found deep in the heart and entrails of India's political economy as it has evolved over the past quarter century.

The short answer to the question is that with deregulation and liberalization, the state has played a different kind of role to the one it played earlier, providing access to scarce public resources as part of a process of promoting private sector-led growth at any cost and supporting without inhibition the omnipresence and play of private interests within the public sphere; and there is plenty of evidence to show that corruption tends to be greater when pro-business strategies of governments bring on or facilitate crony capitalism and 'when there is a state-engineered redistribution of wealth in favour of a few and at the explicit or implicit expense of the many'[14].

A political reckoning over burgeoning levels of corruption was due and it took place with a certain inevitability. Given the unprecedented levels of corruption witnessed over the previous decade, it was no surprise that the issue figured prominently in the 2014 Lok Sabha elections and was responsible, in no small measure, for the rout of the Congress-led United Progressive Alliance (UPA).

TWO

THE MULTIFARIOUSNESS OF CORRUPTION

Corruption in the real world exhibits a remarkable multiplicity of types and forms, with 'a variegated incidence in different times at different places, with varying degrees of damaging consequences'[1]. Many of these types and forms, such as bribery, embezzlement, misappropriation, and influence trading, are common to almost all the 195 countries in the world. Some appear to be distinctive and special to a country or to a set of countries with a shared geography and history. Particular forms of corruption may be endemic in one region within a country but not in another. Other types of corruption, such as money laundering, the sheltering of illegally generated black money in secretive offshore tax havens, and bribery by companies from leading economies doing business abroad have a transnational character.

Corruption and Black Money

Let us consider the relationship between corruption and the generation of black money and income in the specific case of India. Corruption is inextricably intertwined with the black economy, although it would be a conceptual mistake to treat them as being synonymous. As Kumar[2] observes, while 'black income generation and corruption are not synonymous...they do have a two-way relationship. As corruption increases so does the size of the black economy and vice versa. The increase in corruption correlates well with independent estimates that the size of the black economy is growing'. There are various estimates of the size of India's black economy, with Kumar[3] estimating it to be no less than 62 per cent of GDP and other scholars putting it around 25 per cent. Whatever estimate we go by, it is evident that the two-way relationship between corruption and black income generation constitutes a central problem of India's political economy.

Arms Trade Corruption

Worldwide, the arms trade has become synonymous with bribery and influence-peddling under cover of national security. Estimated to account for more than 40 per cent of all corruption in legal international trade[4], arms trade corruption survives and flourishes on the back of collusion among states, developed as well as developing, the industry, and middlemen. The pervasiveness and high levels of arms trade corruption in India—the world's sixth largest military spender among countries, with an estimated military expenditure of $51.3 billion in 2015, accounting for 2.3 per cent of GDP[5]—are well recognized.

Corporate Fraud

Private sector fraud, which rarely figures in mainstream media and public discourse on corruption, must be recognized as one of its most widely prevalent and toxic forms. The Harshad Mehta security scam of 1992 and the Ketan Parekh stock market manipulation scam of 2001 exposed an extensive network of delinquent regulators, politicians, bureaucrats, mutual funds, and banks who had enabled and, in several cases, connived with the central actors, the speculators and brokers, in shaping these spectacular mega-scandals. No worthwhile lessons seem to have been learnt from the experience of dealing with these scams; on the contrary, as Debashis Basu and Sucheta Dalal observe in their insightful book *The Scam*, regulatory and investigative agencies like the Reserve Bank of India, the Central Bureau of Investigation, the Income Tax Department, and the Enforcement Directorate have continued to 'collect evidence and then can it. That emboldens the market players until things go out of hand again'[6].

As we have noted, the first two decades of the twenty-first century have seen corporate and private sector scams surfacing with increasing frequency and on an escalating scale. If the magnitudes of the Harshad Mehta and Ketan Parekh scams were estimated at ₹5,000 crore and ₹6,500 crore respectively, the Satyam Computer Services, Telgi Stamp, Sahara India Pariwar Investor, and Sarada Group Chit Fund scandals featured multiples of those numbers. But more than these spectacular scams, it is the endemic, pervasive, and deepening nature of corruption in the corporate sector that calls for special attention. Several surveys conducted by professional agencies in recent years have come up with independent findings that confirm the impression that corporate fraud has been on the rise in India. Let us look at what three major surveys conducted between 2014 and 2017 reveal.

A survey done in 2014 by the Associated Chambers of Commerce of India (ASSOCHAM) in partnership with the audit, tax, and advisory firm Grant Thornton found that 'Indian corporate frauds arising out of corruption, money laundering, tax evasion, window dressing, financial reporting fraud, and bribery have increased by over 45 per cent' in the preceding two years. The corporate sectors most vulnerable to fraud were identified as real estate and infrastructure, and financial services. What was even worse, more than 70 per cent of the respondents believed that corporate fraud would continue to rise over the next five years[7].

A global fraud survey of senior company executives conducted in early 2015 by the Economist Intelligence Unit for the risk consultancy firm Kroll Inc. found that

India had 'one of the largest fraud problems of any of the countries covered in this report', with an astonishing 80 per cent of the companies covered by the survey 'affected by fraud' in 2015-2016 (compared with 69 per cent in 2013-2014). The areas of frequent loss were identified as corruption and bribery, vendor, supplier, or procurement fraud, and regulatory or compliance breaches. 'The outlook for the future', the India overview in the report concluded, 'is also worrying', with 92 per cent of the Indian respondents reporting that their companies had seen exposure to fraud rise in the preceding year[8].

Another fraud survey, covering Europe, West Asia, India, and Africa, done in 2017 by the market research company Ipsos MORI for Ernst & Young (EY), the global advisory, auditing, and business consultancy firm, reported that 41 per cent of Indian respondents would be prepared to act unethically to enhance their own career progression or remuneration package; 58 per cent stated that loyalty towards their companies prevented employees from reporting fraud, bribery, or corruption; and 78 per cent said bribery and corruption were widespread. These percentages were significantly higher than the corresponding numbers for most of the forty-one countries and territories covered by the survey[9].

Runaway Electoral Funding

Electoral finance typically involves corruption on a large scale. But the variability of national laws regulating campaign financing and donations to political parties and the seriousness with which they are enforced can make a significant difference to the incidence, forms, and scale of this type of corruption. As important are the variable political traditions, social values, and practices among countries. These may facilitate the cruder forms of vote-buying and other corrupt political behaviour—or keep them away or in check.

Against this background, let us briefly look at India's experience in conducting democratic elections. The Election Commission of India (ECI) has been widely praised for its organizational ability, its role in facilitating relatively high voter turnouts, and its success in containing electoral violence. It is equally widely recognized that this constitutional authority, which is charged by Article 324 of the Constitution with the task of 'superintendence, direction and control of elections', has completely failed to prevent the corruption of the electoral process through flagrant violations of legal spending limits involving vast stocks of unaccounted money. A study conducted by the Centre for Media Studies (CMS) ahead of the 2014 Lok Sabha election projected that political parties, candidates, and the government would spend an aggregated ₹30,000 crore on the election[10]. A subsequent study done by CMS during the Lok Sabha election estimated that the total spend on all elections between 2010 and 2014 over the past five years exceeded ₹150,000 crore, half of which came from unaccounted money[11].

Political Finance

However, it would be unfair to hold the ECI accountable for the larger problem of political finance, which features corruption and illegality on a massive scale year-round. Political finance is a deep-seated part of India's political economy and deserves a book in itself. Recent changes in the rules of the game, which make it easier, not more difficult, for companies and high net worth families and individuals to contribute larger, unlimited amounts to political parties in an opaque and 'protected' way make this subject topical as well as interesting.

Meanwhile, what A. P. Mukherjee[12], a former director of the Central Bureau of Investigation (CBI), recounts from an informal conversation he had with Prime Minister Rajiv Gandhi in June 1989, at the height of the Bofors scandal, is of great interest to students of political finance and corruption. When the police officer raised the sensitive issue of the 'atrocious' things people were saying about the Prime Minister's and his family's involvement in Bofors, Rajiv Gandhi responded coolly and matter-of-factly as follows:

> Mr. Mukherjee, you may perhaps imagine that a big all-India party like ours does need substantial amounts of money just for its routine administration throughout the year. This requirement assumes a huge proportion on the eve of Assembly and/or Parliamentary elections. This leads to massive fund collections by important party functionaries all over

the country, which leads to an almost unbreakable unholy *quid pro quo* nexus between unscrupulous party functionaries, ministers, and businessmen.

The Prime Minister explained that he could sense this when he was the Congress party's general secretary and even when he was a youth leader who had entered the political arena reluctantly. What he had to say after that must have shocked Mukherjee to the core. As the former CBI chief recalled the conversation nearly a quarter century later:

> After becoming the Prime Minister towards the end of 1984, he came to know that some senior officers of the armed forces had been surreptitiously collecting huge amounts of money as 'commissions' in respect of most of the defence purchases, quite often in connivance with some ministers, middlemen and civilian officers as well. Though it was in public knowledge for long, no serious or systematic attempt was made to put a stop to such a continuing malady.

So what did Rajiv Gandhi do, according to his own admission? He sought counsel from some of his trusted colleagues and advisers. A suggestion came up that 'all commissions as payable or usually paid to middlemen should be banned but the commissions to be given as matter of routine practice by the suppliers of major defence materials could be pooled under the care of some non-government entity which could be utilised solely for the purpose of meeting the inescapable expenses of the party'. The Prime Minister confirmed to the senior police officer that he had bought into this proposal on the reasoning that 'such a step would largely prevent the collusive nexus between the middlemen, ministers, and bureaucrats' and would enable the government to 'do away with the quid pro quo relationship with some unscrupulous businessmen and equally unscrupulous politicians and bureaucrats'.

This remarkable conversation and admission provides context to what happened in Bofors—and to what *The Hindu* discovered in its investigation of that scandal.

Grand, Petty, and Political Corruption

Anti-corruption campaigners generally fit the multiplicity of types and forms into one of two descriptive boxes—grand corruption and petty or everyday corruption.

Grand corruption is described by Transparency International (TI) as 'acts of corruption committed at a high level of government that distort policies or the central functioning of the state, enabling leaders to benefit at the expense of the public good'. Some scholars who approach the subject of grand corruption from the vantage point of rent-seeking theory break it down into three types—*regulatory*, *extractive*, and *political* (for example, Milan Vaishnav[13]).

Petty corruption is simpler to comprehend: TI describes it as the 'everyday abuse of entrusted power by low- and mid-level public officials in their interactions with ordinary citizens, who often are trying to access basic goods or services in places like hospitals, schools, police departments and other agencies'.

Political corruption, as we have already noted, is described as 'a manipulation of policies, institutions, and rules of procedure in the allocation of resources and financing by political decision-makers, who abuse their position to sustain their power, status, and wealth'.

Bureaucratic corruption, which is treated extensively in the economics literature, is often approached as a distinct category in political studies. But while the differentiation can be significant in some cases, political and bureaucratic corruption are frequently 'interlocked'[14]. This nexus can be observed clearly in India.

A grand corruption case where the nexus between a powerful politician with criminal antecedents and a plethora of officials at various levels can be observed in the Uttar Pradesh food grains scam starring Food Minister Raghuraj Pratap Singh alias Raja Bhaiya and involving the administrators of the state's public distribution system. A CBI investigation found that in one district, Sitapur, 100 per cent of the food meant for the poor was stolen between 2005 and 2007[15]. According to an affidavit filed in the Delhi High Court by a whistle-blower, a former aide to the Food Minister, the minister's wife allegedly received $20 million over an eighteen-month period between 2005 and 2007[16]. *Bloomberg News* compiled data that showed that the value of the food grain missing for the ten years ending 2012 was $14.5 billion[17]. The fruits of this grand embezzlement scheme were shared from bottom to top on a rising scale. Citing a CBI investigating officer, the *Bloomberg* article explained the modus operandi of the scandal as follows: 'Often using dummy firms, local officials paid the national government the subsidised prices for the food—as little as one-tenth of the market rate—then sold it to private companies at market prices and pocketed the difference. Poor Indians seeking rations at their local Fair Price Shop would find a locked door...or be told to "buzz off" and return the following month.'[18]

Decentralization and Corruption

Political corruption is usually bracketed with grand corruption, but must not be treated as synonymous with it. Aside from being a conceptual mistake, doing so would result in a seriously flawed diagnosis of, and prescription against, the deep-seated malaise. It is easy to see that political as much as bureaucratic decision-makers can be corrupt at a non-grand, local, or 'petty' level. They can abuse, at their level and in highly damaging ways, entrusted power for private gain even while being uninvolved in the making of state and central government policy or in the functioning of the state and central governments.

An interesting example from India is the local-level corruption system in Uttar Pradesh that was meticulously observed and documented by Charan Singh (1902-1987), a well-educated and shrewd, if opportunist, politician who valued his personal integrity and, quite adventitiously, towards the end of his career was installed as prime minister for six months in 1979-1980. The Charan Singh papers, an illuminating private archive to which the political scientist Paul Brass was given unrestricted access, reveal that corruption was endemic to the system even before Independence and was 'entangled…in the very roots of Indian society, in all its local conflicts from village to town, district, and state.'[19]

In recent years, the link between decentralization and corruption across India has become a productive area of interdisciplinary research and news reporting. This is an area where political and sociological studies as well as investigative journalism can work with the insights offered by the economics literature on decentralized, as distinct from centralized, corruption. Bardhan argues that 'with decentralisation and devolution of authority to [elected] local sub-provincial governments, corruption may increase if proximity makes capture of local governments by the locally powerful people easier than in the case of higher-level authorities'[20]. Siphoning off cash and kind, at local points of delivery, from the large resources allotted by the central and state governments to anti-poverty programmes is now recognized as a systematized mode of corruption. *Battling Corruption: Has NREGA Reached India's Rural Poor?* by Shylashri Shankar and Raghav Gaiha, a well-designed study of the effectiveness of formal and informal mechanisms in reducing corruption in the administration of the National Rural Employment Guarantee Act (NREGA) scheme, and in enhancing the welfare of the rural poor, throws up a mixed, but on the whole, distressing picture of systematically stealing from the entitlements of the poorest of the rural poor, especially when they are illiterate, least socially networked, lower caste, and landless[21].

In a country as big, diverse, and populous as India, the aggregated corruption through the exercise of political power at the decentralized, local levels can be staggeringly high, an enormous drain on resources meant to go into productive activity and welfare. To acknowledge this is not to argue against either the federal political system or the 73rd and 74th constitutional amendments, which systematized and empowered local government in rural and urban areas respectively. However, to treat what happens at the decentralized, local levels of the state and political economy as petty corruption would be a serious conceptual mistake, with damaging implications for policymaking and politics.

News Media Corruption and Sharp Practices

Finally, we come to the issue of pervasive corruption in the news media industry, which no commentary on corruption can ignore if it is to be credible. The best known and the most flagrant form of corruption in the press and in news television is the practice that has come to be known as 'paid news'. P. Sainath offers this handy definition: 'Paid news is run to pass off an advertisement, a piece of propaganda and advertisement...as news... Paid news does not discloset to the reader that this information has been paid for.'[22]

The issue exploded in the public sphere in the aftermath of the 2009 general election. A section of the press revealed that many newspapers, big, medium-sized, and small, and several news television channels had sold promotional news packages of specified size, using an under-the-table rate card, to candidates in state assembly and parliamentary elections. Candidates who could not pay, or refused to pay, were blotted out of news coverage. There were special rates for negative coverage of the candidates' opponents. Paid news involved violations of the election law, was tantamount to extortion in several cases, and mocked every rule of ethical journalism. It was every bit of a rogue practice as the UK's phone hacking affair was. The scandal of paid news led to a damning report by a subcommittee of the Press Council of India[23], a sanitized version of this report released by the Council[24], and calls for external regulation of the press and the private news television channels.

The PCI subcommittee's report pulled no punches:

> Corruption in the mass media in India...is as old as the media itself. If there is corruption in society, it would be unrealistic to expect the media to be free of corruption.... In recent years, corruption in the Indian media has gone way beyond the corruption of individual journalists and specific

> media organisations—from planting information and views in lieu of favours received in cash or kind, to more institutionalised and organised forms of corruption wherein newspapers and television channels receive funds for publishing or broadcasting information in favour of particular individuals, corporate entities, representatives of political parties and candidates contesting elections, that is sought to be disguised as news...The phenomenon of 'paid news'...has become pervasive, structured and highly organised and, in the process, is undermining democracy in India.

Thanks to the exposés of 2009-2010, paid news as an issue has gained visibility within the news industry and in politics, with working journalists' associations and the Editors' Guild of India expressing concern and placing it on their agenda and with the Election Commission of India issuing instructions and detailed guidelines to chief electoral officers of states and union territories to look out for paid news at the time of elections and adopt strict measures to check this corrupt and illegal practice. It needs to be added that such concern and vigilance are limited to paid news in election season, when detecting and acting against the practice is relatively simple.

However, as the PCI subcommittee report notes, corruption in India's news media is not confined to paid news published or broadcast at the time of election campaigns. Paid news is a deeper, wider, industry-wide practice that takes place round the year in collusion with the corporate sector, politicians, and special interests. But this is not all. The rapid growth of the Indian news industry since the early 1990s must be viewed as a positive development, especially because in consequence the reach and influence of journalism, some of it very good, has grown in politics and society. But this upturn in the fortunes of the industry has been accompanied by the intensification and spread of corruption and various negative trends that challenge the self-proclaimed core, democratic values of the news media.

Increasing concentration of ownership in some media sectors; higher levels of manipulation of news, analysis, and comment to suit the owners' financial and political interests; the downgrading and devaluing of editorial functions and content in some leading media organizations; the systematic and cynical dumbing down of content, led by the nose by certain types of market research; the growing willingness of media organizations to tailor their editorial product to subserve advertising and marketing goals set by owners and senior management; hyper-commercialization; price wars and aggressive practices in the home bases of rivals to overwhelm and kill competition, raising fears about media monopoly; private treaties with corporates that undermine the independence and value of news—these are deeply worrying tendencies[25].

In such a scenario, the lines between corruption and other forms of sharp practice tend to get blurred. But the bottom line is clear enough: suborned news media and compromised journalism cannot play a significant, let alone a leading, role in investigating, exposing, and combating corruption in politics, in the corporate world, and in society.

THREE

LAW AND ENFORCEMENT

Writing in mid-1989, at the height of the Bofors investigation, Upendra Baxi explored the judicial discourse in the Antulay case—a landmark political corruption case that witnessed 'the destiny of Indian law and jurisprudence' coming into 'direct confrontation with the will to absolute power, in all its manifestations'. Baxi observed that the anti-corruption law operated 'episodically' when it came to top and senior bureaucrats and 'more systematically' in the case of lower officials. He had much to say on the immunity that attached to corruption in high places, in popular belief, legally, and operationally. He presented a systematic analysis of how laws dealing with corruption offences were a causative factor in the scaling up and spread of corruption in India, and how 'constitutional liberties have, operatively, resulted in a system of legal immunity for a bribal culture'[1].

Two significant, and on the face of it far-reaching

and stringent, anti-corruption laws have made their way into the statute books since Baxi registered his angst, as scholar and citizen, in *Liberty and Corruption: The Antulay Case and Beyond*.

The Prevention of Corruption Act 1988[2] supplanted India's first direct and consolidated law to tackle corruption among public servants, the PCA 1947, which had as its stated aim making 'effective provision for the prevention of bribery and corruption' among public servants. The 1947 Act had been amended and a Central Vigilance Commission (CVC) created in 1964 on the basis of the recommendations made two years earlier by the Committee on Prevention of Corruption headed by K. Santhanam. The PCA that is currently in force was introduced as 'an Act to consolidate and amend the law relating to the prevention of corruption and for matters connected therewith'. Interestingly, it came into force on 9 September 1988, when the Rajiv Gandhi government was in big political trouble on account of the rapidly unfolding Bofors kickbacks scandal.

Equally interesting is the fact that the Prevention of Corruption (Amendment) Bill 2013 which was introduced in the Rajya Sabha on 19 August of that year to amend the PCA 1988, as well as two other laws covering corruption offences, came at a time when the United Progressive Alliance government was besieged by a number of major corruption scandals, each one of which, in the magnitude of bribes or kickbacks involved, made Bofors look like small change. The Statement of Objects and Reasons for the amending legislation introduced it as being necessitated by the ratification by India of the United Nations Convention Against Corruption, international practice on the treatment of the offence of bribery and corruption, judicial pronouncements, and the need to amend the PCA 1988 and connected legislation 'so as to fill in gaps in description and coverage of the offence of bribery' and bring India's anti-corruption jurisprudence 'in line with current international practice and also to meet more effectively the country's obligations under the aforesaid Convention'.

Not surprisingly, the bill has taken its time to wend its way through the executive and legislative process, punctuated by references to the Parliament Standing Committee on Personnel, Public Grievances, Law, a Select Committee of the Rajya Sabha, and, following an informal decision of the Cabinet, to the Law Commission of India. In its Report No. 254[3], submitted in the record time of less than a month, the Law Commission under the chairmanship of an outstanding jurist, retired Justice A. P. Shah, suggested the removal of several conceptual and procedural flaws in the bill.

It remains to be seen what final shape this anti-corruption legislation will take. What is evident is that three key provisions of the UN Convention—bribery of foreign public officials, bribery in the private sector, and compensation for those who have suffered damage as a result of an act of corruption—will not be included in the PCA (amendment) legislation[4]. The first set of corruption offences was sought to be covered by a separate bill, which was introduced in the Lok Sabha in 2011 but has lapsed. The second item, bribery in the private sector, may not fall within the ambit of a law meant to combat corruption by public servants but needs to be addressed separately, as India's ratification of the UN Convention demands. But there seems to be no defensible reason for not incorporating the third provision—compensation for those aggrieved by an act of corruption—in legislation meant to tighten and toughen the PCA and further the cause of justice.

A close analysis by PRS Legislative Research of the Prevention of Corruption (Amendment) Bill 2013, which is pending in Parliament, reveals that in significant respects the original anti-corruption law is being diluted rather than strengthened[5]. The bill takes away the protection given by the 1988 Act to a bribe-giver for any statement he makes during a corruption trial, thus introducing a deterrent against giving evidence as a witness. It weakens the provision relating to a public servant's possession of disproportionate assets by introducing a requirement that in addition to possession, the *intention* of the public servant to acquire disproportionate assets must be established, thus 'raising the threshold for proving the offence'. Further, the bill redefines the offence of criminal misconduct by a public servant, narrowing its scope to cover only dishonest and fraudulent misappropriation of property under his control, and intentional illicit enrichment and possession of disproportionate assets. It excises from the offence three circumstances covered by the main act: using illegal means to obtain any valuable thing or monetary reward for himself or any other person; abusing his position as a public servant to do the same; and obtaining for any person a valuable thing or monetary reward without public interest. The requirement of prior sanction from the appropriate authority for the prosecution of public officials will now cover former as well as serving public officials. These amendments point to the non-seriousness of the government, the political establishment, and Parliament in delivering on the promise to tighten and toughen the country's principal anti-corruption law.

The foot-dragging by the Congress-led UPA government and the backsliding by the BJP government over a whistle-blower protection law, which was originally proposed by the Law Commission of India in 2001, tell their own story. The Whistleblowers Protection Bill was adopted by the Lok Sabha in December 2011 and by the Rajya Sabha in February 2014, received presidential assent in May 2014, was sought to be diluted through an amendment bill that is pending in the Rajya Sabha, and is yet to be given effect to. The Whistleblowers Protection Act 2011 (Act No. 17 of 2014)[6], describes itself as legislation to establish a mechanism to 'receive complaints relating to disclosures on any allegation of corruption or wilful misuse of power or wilful misuse of discretion against any public servant and to inquire into such disclosure' while providing adequate safeguards against the victimization of the whistle-blower.

After the bill was adopted by the Lok Sabha, some amendments barring public interest disclosure of information relating to matters such as national security, the strategic, scientific, or economic interests of the state, relations with foreign states, and cabinet proceedings were circulated in the Rajya Sabha in 2013 but they could not be moved before the bill was finally adopted. The Whistleblowers Protection (Amendment) Bill 2015, which was passed by the Lok Sabha in May 2015 and is pending in the Rajya Sabha, goes much further than the earlier attempts to dilute the Act.

Under the 2011 Act anyone can make a public interest disclosure to a competent authority on a public servant's alleged act of corruption, or misuse of power or discretion, or attempt to commit or commission a criminal offence. Further, notwithstanding anything contained in the Official Secrets Act 1923, any person may make a public interest disclosure before the competent authority. The Act specifies the following competent authorities: the prime minister or chief minister for ministers, the speaker or chairman for members of parliament or state legislatures, the chief justice of the high court for subordinate judges, and the central or state vigilance commissions for government servants. The provisions of the Act do not apply to the Special Protection Group and, interestingly, to judges of the high courts and the Supreme Court of India.

The 2015 amendment bill prohibits disclosure to the competent authority of information relating to a public servant's alleged corruption or misuse of power or discretion, or attempt to commit a criminal offence if such disclosure contains information falling under ten broad categories. They include information relating to national security; strategic, scientific or economic interests of the state; friendly relations with foreign states; proceedings of the Council of Ministers; and commercial confidence, trade secrets, and intellectual property. They also include information received in confidence from a foreign government, and information received in a fiduciary capacity. Further, no public interest disclosure of information may be made if it is prohibited under the Official Secrets Act 1923[7].

The Statement of Objects and Reasons of the 2015 Amendment Bill claims that the amendments relating to the ten prohibited categories 'have been modelled on the provisions' of the Right to Information (RTI) Act 2005[8]. However, independent analysts have found the comparison to be inappropriate and indeed misleading, because while 'the purpose of the RTI Act is to make information with public authorities accessible to all citizens to promote transparency and accountability…the Whisleblowers Act provides for corruption-related information to be given by an individual to a Competent Authority'[9].

It is a telling commentary on the importance the government and the political system attach to the fight against corruption that a decade-and-a-half after the Law Commission recommended that whistle-blowing legislation be enacted and even provided a draft for it, a law that has been on the statute book since May 2014 is yet to be notified.

The idea of an ombudsman to enquire into, or investigate, allegations of political corruption has been around for a long time. But it failed to take off the ground. Against this background, the Lokpal and Lokayuktas Act 2013[10], is a significant step forward. It is worth reminding ourselves that the Act was not a voluntary legislative exercise; it was forced on the national political agenda in 2011-2012 by anti-corruption mass movements spearheaded by Anna Hazare and Arvind Kejriwal. What is more, the legislation, which has been in force from January 2014 (and was amended in 2016 to provide for the form and manner in which a public servant is required to declare his or her assets and liabilities), is yet to be operationalized, despite the Supreme Court of India pulling up the government for its indifference towards the issue.

Paralleling the non-seriousness about the whistle-blower law, the inordinate delay in putting in place an ombudsman-like institution—the Lokpal for the union and the Lokayukta for the states—'to enquire into allegations of corruption against certain public functionaries and for matters connected therewith or incidental thereto' reflects poorly on the Indian political system. It seems that the idea of establishing and operationalizing a system of independent investigation and prosecution of corruption offences committed by public servants, including any person who is or has been a minister, a prime minister, a member of parliament, or a senior bureaucrat, is viewed as dangerous radicalism.

But going beyond timelines and delays, how much of an actual advance does the Lokpal as an institution represent? And what are its potentialities in the scheme of anti-corruption jurisprudence and operationalizing effective and speedy criminal action against the corrupt? I posed these questions to a law scholar who has researched this subject. In his emailed response, which is worth quoting in full, N. S. Nigam, Associate Professor at the Azim Premji University in Bengaluru, explained why the Lokpal could not possibly be a deep cure for corruption in India:

> Its proposed strength is its independence from the political corruption that it is supposed to investigate. However, even the most independent of investigative agencies cannot *adjudicate* the guilt of persons accused of corruption. An investigating body cannot establish conclusively that a person is involved in political corruption; in a democracy this function is performed by the judiciary alone. If the judicial process is delayed or compromised in adjudicating on corruption, the Lokpal's efforts will necessarily fail to bear fruition.
>
> Most debates on the Lokpal assume that the anti-corruption regime in India would be transformed once the Lokpal is operational. While the investigative mechanism will be strengthened,

the *Jayalalithaa* judgement is a stark reminder that the most intractable problem in tackling corruption in India lies in the hijacking of the adjudicative process by the lawyers of the accused, and in the failure on the part of the judiciary to observe strict timelines. The *Jayalalithaa* case lingered in the lower courts for eighteen years before it was decided, in no small measure due to the dilatory tactics of the defence lawyers. The Lokpal and Lokayuktas Act has imposed a two-year limit on decisions by the court of first instance in corruption cases but there are no time limits on the High Courts and the Supreme Court, where most corruption cases will reach eventually. In any case, imposing statutory time limits on judicial decisions is an area that has not received proper scrutiny in India. Without resolving the issue of judicial delays, India cannot hope to dent corruption through the Lokpal alone.[11]

Two large and separate issues are highlighted here. One is the non-seriousness of the government and most political parties in giving practical effect to the Lokpal legislation. The other issue is the intractable problem of the law's delays, which featuring the frequent 'hijacking of the adjudicative process' by defence lawyers and the failure of the judiciary to observe strict timelines, ensures that even if the investigation is independent and efficient, the corrupt in high places cannot be tried and punished within anything like a reasonable time-frame.

It is too much to expect the notion of immunity for the politically powerful from investigation, prosecution, and adjudication of corruption offences to go away without a fight. The immunity attaching to political corruption at the bar of public prosecution may be somewhat less than it was a quarter century ago, but there is little empirical evidence to suggest that the effective immunity has gone away. From time to time, ministers at the central or state level facing allegations of corruption have been obliged to resign. Some ministers and ex-ministers, and several legislators and middle-ranking and senior bureaucrats have faced investigation, prosecution, and trial under the PCA, and there have been a few convictions. But since these legal processes invariably go on for many years and convictions can be appealed, nothing can stop the out-on-bail netas from returning to the thick of political battle with renewed vigour.

What is striking is that despite the flagrant way and the massive scale on which corruption takes place across India, so little is being done to go after the big fish. Even as the Supreme Court has come up with orders, directions, and obiter dicta aimed at the evils of corruption, the scale of political corruption appears to be growing exponentially.

From anti-corruption laws, let us now turn to enforcement. Looking for underlying drivers of corruption in India, Sukhtankar and Vaishnav put their finger on the lack of enforcement capacity as one of the two 'deep' causes, the other being the old chestnut, 'regulatory complexity'[12]. The two 'proximate' causes they identify are poor regulation of political finance, and shortcomings in public sector recruitment and postings. The researchers attribute the lack of enforcement capacity to such factors as the 'overburdened, inadequately staffed and often poorly equipped' government agencies in charge of administration and law and order; the small number of government employees relative to population and the enormous burdens placed on them to enforce the very large number of schemes and regulations in place; political interference and meddling; unfilled job vacancies, especially in the police services and in courts (from the subordinate to the High Court level); and the unmanageable backlog of cases that has clogged up the judicial system.

It may come as a surprise that among the Group of Twenty (G20) countries, India has the smallest number of government employees in relation to the national population. The administrative services are overburdened at all levels. These statistics provided by Sukhtankar and Vaishnav are revealing. The country has 146 public sector employees per 10,000 residents, compared with 537 for China, 730 for the United States and Germany, and 1,534 in Russia. It has the lowest ratio of police officers—122.5 per 10,000 people—of any G20 country. It has 16.5 judges per million residents compared with 101 for the United States. While the vacancy rate in the police 'veers on the alarming...for certain states', including India's most populous state, Uttar Pradesh, the massive case backlog compounded by the high rates of judicial vacancies in the high courts and district and subordinate courts 'induces despair'[13].

The preliminary findings, released in 2016, of a study by the Commonwealth Human Rights Initiative(CHRI) of what happens to corruption cases across India reveal a shocking picture of the political-legal system's apathy towards these offences. The research, covering the period 2001-2015, drew on data published by the National Crime Record Bureau (NCRB) and released as machine-readable and machine-analysable datasets on an open digital platform of the National Informatics Centre. The objectives of the study were to provide 'a snapshot view' of the action taken by states and union territories on corruption-related offences; to compare the incidence of corruption with other major offences; and to demonstrate the value of using open datasets to examine the anti-corruption actions of the government.

The CHRI study revealed that over the fifteen-year period corruption cases accounted for a near invisible 0.06 per cent of 91.1 million registered criminal crimes, including murder, kidnapping and abduction, and robbery. Only 54,139 cases of corruption were registered compared with 116,010 reports of bribes paid posted on just one website 'I Paid a Bribe'. A comparison of the NCRB datasets revealed that ten cases of murder, eleven cases of kidnapping or abduction, and six cases of robbery were registered across the country for one registered case of corruption. 'This comparison', the CHRI report comments, 'seems to indicate [a] severe lack of public confidence in the ability of the anti-corruption agencies to investigate a complaint of corruption, collect evidence, and put the case up for trial'[14].

But the failure of enforcement goes beyond this. The study found that the trial was completed in 55.26 per cent of the 54,139 registered cases of corruption but only 35.33 per cent of the cases that were sent to trial ended in conviction. But the most telling statistic was that merely 19.53 per cent of all registered corruption cases ended in conviction. The picture varied across states but that is not material for this discussion. What the preliminary findings of CHRI's research tell us is that enforcement of the anti-corruption laws figures among the lowest priorities of India's political-legal system.

SECTION II

HISTORY, DEFINITIONS, AND THEORY

FOUR

'ASIATIC CORRUPTION' AND THE SCANDAL OF EMPIRE

Just as it is impossible to know when a fish moving in water is drinking it, so it is impossible to find out when government servants in charge of undertakings misappropriate money.

—Kautilya, *The Arthashastra*, Part VI, 2.9.33

What, then, shall become of us, if Bengal, if the Ganges pour in a new tide of corruption? Should the evil genius of British liberty so ordain it, I fear this House will be so far from removing the corruption of the East, that it will be corrupted by them. I dread more from the infection of that place, than I hope from your virtue.

—Edmund Burke in the House of Commons, 1772

Edmund Burke was an eloquent and powerful critic of empire... In the end, Burke's real legacy was the transformation of Company rule into British imperium. Through his role in shaping the reforms and then in impeaching Hastings, he managed to rescue the imperial mission, transforming corruption into virtue, private malfeasance into public good, mercantile disgrace into national triumph.

—Nicholas B. Dirks, *The Scandal of Empire*, 2007

No country, region, province, or locality is free from corruption. The significant differences across the world lie in the degree of its prevalence and pervasiveness; its morphology; its effects; and the capability and willingness of nation states and their enforcement and other legal institutions, with support from an alert public, to prevent corruption and crack down on it when it occurs.

The importance of history to a deeper, better contextualized, and more nuanced understanding of corruption, and the question of why the incidence of corruption varies significantly across time and place, cannot be overemphasized. An issue of some theoretical as well as practical importance is how to transform a 'historical initial condition' of high corruption in which a society or country may be 'locked in' into a position of low corruption[1]. Ranking India at the time of Independence on an international scale of high to low corruption would be a virtually impossible task. However, despite the strong opposition to all forms of corruption shown by the leaders of the freedom struggle, above all Mohandas Karamchand Gandhi, we can reasonably assume Brass's assertion that corruption was endemic to the system even before Independence and was 'entangled in the very roots of Indian society…in all its local conflicts from village to town, district, and state' to be the real state of affairs. What needs to be added is that the colonial contribution to, and complicity in, this state of affairs was massive.

An influential theme in British imperialist historiography is the pervasiveness, inescapability, and deeply malign influence of 'Asiatic corruption'. In the case of India, this was seen and repeatedly depicted as the culturally, socially, and historically predetermined general condition of the country, incurable without imperium. In 1772, Clive concluded his defence in the House of Commons against accusations of personal corruption with a boast about his importance as the founding genius of a great sovereign power and his integrity in comparison with corrupt East India Company colleagues in a historical context where the giving and receiving of 'presents' was customary:

> A great prince was dependent on my pleasure, an opulent city lay at my mercy; its richest bankers bid against each other for my smiles; I walked through vaults which were thrown open to me alone, piled on either hand with gold and jewels! Mr. Chairman, at this moment I stand astonished at my own moderation.[2]

There can be little question that the giving and receiving of costly presents in exchange for, or in anticipation of, favours, and corruption in many other forms were deeply entrenched and pervasive in India during the eighteenth century—and before and after that as well.

But as Nicholas Dirks shows in his illuminating historical study of *The Scandal of Empire*, which has as its central reference point the impeachment of Warren Hastings, while there was a scandal about the servants of the company, the nabobs, carrying back with them 'the fruits of this Asiatic corruption', the higher order scandal was the Company itself: 'What was supposed to have been a trading company with an eastern monopoly vested by Parliament had become a rogue state: waging war, administering justice, minting coin, and collecting revenue over Indian territory.'[3]

The scandal of conquest, violence, and oppression; the wholesale loot of national resources; the enormous drain on the country's wealth; the misuse of grants, agreements, and treaties; fraud, forgery, and malfeasance of every kind; judicial murder; the predatory assertion of absolute sovereignty; a generalized system of grand corruption; and ideological justification and casuistry—this was the real imperial story. It can be reasonably surmised from the historical evidence that the Asiatic corruption encountered by Company functionaries and later British rulers in India, including the so-called reformers, was more than matched, in fact, was vastly surpassed and eclipsed, by the scandal of empire. This only goes to show that the lines between corruption and other ways of scamming people are often blurred.

For all the modernizing and civilizing claims made by apologists of the imperialist British Raj, and notwithstanding the vaunted personal financial integrity of some Governors-General and viceroys and several members of the Indian Civil Service (ICS), the institutional arrangements, legal instruments, rules of the game, and ingrained practices which, in independent India, have effectively shielded corrupt politicians and bureaucrats and also big business interests involved in corruption from serious investigation and prosecution owe a great deal to the Raj.

It would be grossly unjust to pin the label of Asiatic corruption on the leaders, the next-level activists, and the overwhelming majority of foot soldiers of India's freedom struggle. Nevertheless, as we will see in the next chapter, there is credible evidence from the early years of Independence that at least in some regions, corruption was endemic to the system and society at various levels.

The controversies over political corruption in the first decade-and-a-half of Independence did not amount to much, at least not by latter-day standards. Take for instance the Jeep scandal, which played out between 1948 and 1955, and the Mundhra scandal, which raged on the political stage in 1957-1958. The first involved V. K. Krishna Menon, India's High Commissioner in the United Kingdom, and the charge against him was that he had ignored the laid-down procedure in signing a ₹80 lakh contract with a foreign firm for the purchase of army jeeps. The second and more serious case involved the sale of fictitious shares by Haridas Mundhra, a Calcutta-based businessman, to the Life Insurance Corporation, causing a loss of ₹1.25 crore to the latter. This led to the resignation of Finance Minister T. T. Krishnamachari, after a commission of inquiry held that a minister must take full responsibility for the actions of his subordinates and must not be allowed to get away by saying they did not reflect his policy or acted contrary to his directions. It was no one's case that either Krishna Menon or Krishnamachari had been bribed or had personally benefitted from the transactions or the arbitrary decisions made.

One question that surfaces now and again, in subtle as well as crude forms, is whether Indian society is more hospitable to corruption than most other societies, whether Indians as a people are more predisposed to be corrupt than most other peoples. I have already noted that more than two centuries ago the founders and apologists of British empire in India raised and answered this question affirmatively, in evocative terms; and that the label 'Asiatic corruption' stuck, producing over time many iterations of the colonialist point of view of Indian society as incurably corrupt. But the question does not become invalid just because of the predatory historical circumstances in which it first came to the fore.

So is India more corrupt than most other countries? When it comes to comparisons, there is an easy case and a virtually insoluble one. What we can say with certainty or near certainty, based on our general knowledge and experience, is that there is far more corruption in India than in Denmark or the United Kingdom or Germany or Singapore. This is a subjective, qualitative judgement that is easy to form and it is unlikely to be contested seriously. But is there more corruption in India than in China or South Africa or Brazil or Nigeria? We cannot answer this question because there is no reliable empirical basis on which quantitative comparisons of corruption can be made, and qualitative judgements can be no more than guesses.

Nevertheless, given the 'internationalisation of the question of corruption' in recent decades[4], inter-country comparisons and rankings are regularly served up. In 2016, India ranked 79th, tying with Belarus, Brazil, and China, among 176 countries and territories covered by Transparency International's Corruption Perception Index (CPI)[5]. The country's ranking had worsened by three places from its 2015 position.

But does this mean that India in 2016 was more corrupt than all the seventy-six countries and territories ranking above it? Or less corrupt than every one of the ninety-four ranking below it? Not necessarily, because for a start the CPI, the best-known indicator of corruption worldwide, which has been coming out annually in some form since 1995, is a subjective exercise that involves variables that are extremely hard to control and systematize for analysis. Transparency International's annual index ranks countries not by estimating the absolute levels of corruption occurring on the basis of hard empirical data[6], but by drawing from several sources to come up with a composite index of how corrupt a country's public sector is perceived to be. The CPI admits to relying heavily on the perceptions of business people and country experts.

The various data sources that feed into the CPI do not concern themselves seriously with how ordinary people feel, probably because they do not wish to engage with the folklore of corruption. Given this basic limitation of the exercise, does a small rise or fall in the annual rankings signal an improvement or a worsening in the actual level of corruption? They do not, because for a start India's CPI ranking in 2016 relative to 2015 or 2014 is affected by the performance, over the same period, of other countries on the list. A somewhat more meaningful indicator is the perceptions-based integrity score of a country over, say, a five-year period and this is available in the CPI: India's average for the period 2012-2016 is a dismal 37.6 (on a scale of 0 to 100 where zero is the highest level of perceived corruption and 100 the lowest) compared with 90.8 and 90 for top-ranked Denmark and New Zealand.

But there is something else about the CPI that regularly escapes the attention and critical scrutiny of the mainstream media, which find that the annual rankings can make good headlines. The most striking limitation of Transparency International's exercise is not that it is perception-based, or even that it relies overwhelmingly on the perceptions of business people and country experts. It is that it confines itself to corruption in the public sector, overlooking the massive role played by the private sector, corporate as well as other business interests, in corruption. This is the main reason why radical critics regard the CPI more as an ideological exercise targeted at developing countries than as a genuine attempt to get the measure of corruption worldwide[7].

In 1999, Transparency International did make a foray into a new area with its Bribe Payers Index. This attempted to capture 'the supply side of international bribery' by ranking the likelihood of companies from several leading economies to pay bribes when doing business abroad. The Bribe Payers Index 2011[8], the most recent in the series, ranks twenty-eight of the world's leading economies according to the likelihood of their paying bribes to win business abroad. The index is based on a survey of business executives as captured by Transparency International's 2011 Bribe Payers Survey. Interestingly, the Netherlands and Switzerland top the list of countries reported as least likely to pay such bribes while the United Kingdom, the United States, and France rank 8, 10, and 11 respectively among the twenty-eight. But despite such exercises, pursuit of the supply side of international bribery has not gained much traction in the realm of national laws and state policy, for reasons that stem largely from ideology and realpolitik.

Journalistic investigations have turned up quite a lot of evidence that, as a rule, multinationals transacting business abroad do engage in large-scale corruption. They do this either proactively, that is, by controlling the situation to win a bid, establish or expand facilities, pursue a competitive advantage, or change government regulations and policy, or reactively, that is, by falling in line with demands for bribes to ministers and other public officials. There are exceptions but they are extremely hard to identify, since foreign companies and business executives who refuse to pay bribes when they are demanded are invariably silent on the matter, possibly from fear of controversy and even reprisals.

There are sectors such as mining and, most notoriously the arms trade, where many foreign companies trying to do business with India engage in corruption, almost always through intermediaries or middlemen. Disguising bribes and kickbacks as commissions and routing them through agents to decision-makers seems to be the rule rather than the exception. 'In the Indian economy', Josy Joseph, an investigative journalist, observes in his book, *A Feast of Vultures*, 'middlemen play out their roles in the dingy back rooms of decision making. They carry bribes, pay whoever needs to be paid, intimidate someone if required, and ensure that their clients have insider information on a contract from the very beginning of the process. They provide undue and unfair advantage.'[9] In all these cases, it is pointless even to ask the question: who is more culpable, the giver or the receiver of the bribes? They must be treated as equally culpable.

Transparency International's Bribe Payers Index may not place the United Kingdom among the countries that are most likely to pay bribes to win or further business abroad. On the face of it, the UK Bribery Act 2010[10], which entered into force in July 2011, is one of the toughest anti-corruption laws in the world. It provides for prosecution and penalties for both 'active' and 'passive' bribery, including bribery of foreign public officials and various related offences committed overseas. The penalties include imprisonment up to a maximum of ten years, an unlimited fine, and confiscation of property. The Act also enhances the risk of prosecution for a company or partnership if it fails to have in place 'adequate procedures' to prevent bribery by any person associated with it. But the way the cases of BAE Systems[11], a British defence, security, and aerospace multinational, and Rolls-Royce[12], a global leader in manufacturing, among other things, engines for military as well as commercial large aircraft, have been settled with the prosecuting authorities in 2010 and 2017 respectively is instructive. These cases have been well documented and there is no need to go into details here. It is enough to note that the two multinationals have faced a string of allegations of corruption and wrongdoing in their business operations worldwide, including in India; have admitted guilt in several cases; have had to pay heavy fines and costs running into hundreds of millions of dollars; but considering the scale of wrongdoing they were engaged in over long periods have got away relatively lightly in the eyes of many independent observers.

The U. S. Foreign Corrupt Practices Act (FCPA), which provides for fines and imprisonment for specified offences, is supposed to act as a deterrent to the supply side of bribery of foreign officials by US citizens and entities doing business abroad. But it has loopholes dictated by policy and realpolitik and there are enough indications that this legislation is honoured in the breach from time to time. The September 2016 'voluntary' regulatory filings on suspected corruption involving its Indian facilities by

Cognizant Technology Solutions Corp., a relatively well-regarded information technology, consulting, and business process services multinational, to the US Securities and Exchange Commission (SEC) and the US Department of Justice, suggested that the violations were serious[13]. In its annual report for fiscal 2016, filed with the SEC on 1 March 2017, Cognizant, which is highly dependent on its foreign operations and has the majority of its delivery centres and no fewer than 188,000 of its 260,200 employees located in India, disclosed that 'in 2016, we incurred $27 million in costs related to the FCPA investigation and related lawsuits'[14]. It stated further that the outcome of the internal investigation being conducted under the oversight of its Audit Committee, with the assistance of outside counsel, into possible violations of the FCPA and other similar laws and related litigation 'could have a material adverse effect on our business, annual and interim results of operations, cash flows and financial condition'.

All this underlines the need for law enforcement to be more vigilant, more energetic, and more effective in investigating and prosecuting foreign companies when they violate Indian laws as well as the laws of their own countries while doing business in India. If law enforcement, which is subject to political supervision and control, is reluctant or unable to act on its own, it can be made to act by the pressure of informed public opinion or, in certain cases, by judicial intervention brought on by public interest litigation. Whether he succeeds in his public-spirited endeavour or not, Prashant Bhushan's letter of 7 March 2017 to CBI Director Alok Kumar Verma demanding that a criminal case be filed against Rolls-Royce in light of a January 2017 order of the Crown Court, London, that is favourable to India shows the way forward[15].

FIVE

CONCEPTUALIZING AND DEFINING CORRUPTION

Getting a handle on corruption is not as easy as the folklore makes it out to be.

It is useful here to make a distinction between the approach taken by classical economic theory to the conceptualization of corruption and the seemingly less tolerant and more judgmental approaches encountered in political studies and in the socio-political arena.

As Bardhan, who has extensively researched the subject of corruption, puts it:

> Almost everyone is exercised about the pervasive problem of corruption in much of the world, but while most people, including other social scientists, emphasise values and ethics in this context, economists usually take a different approach, emphasising the need for appropriate incentives and punishments instead.[1]

He points out, further, that the notion of corruption most often used by economists—the 'use of public office for private gain'—misses out an important dimension of corruption, the 'abuse of private office for private gain' and here too the public sector is implicated in the sense that it has been 'lax in the regulations that were supposed to restrain the activities of private actors'. Another limitation of the literature in economics is that much of it is about bureaucratic corruption while political corruption is rarely studied[2].

On the face of it, the divergence in purpose, scope, and method is so striking that it is easy to conclude that there can be no meeting point between the two broad approaches. Nevertheless, the question whether a bridge exists, or can be built, between the insights, analyses, and prescriptions that classical economic theory on the one hand, and other social sciences on the other, offer on the nature, determinants, effects, and tameability of corruption is relevant and needs to be examined with an open mind.

Corruption in the Literature of Economics

Economists have traditionally discussed the phenomenon of corruption in terms of a principal–agent model[3]. Typically, this features a benevolent principal, a misbehaving agent violating set rules and colluding with third parties for private gain, the principal finding it difficult to monitor the activity of the agent, and the resultant welfare costs. But over time this approach has been found to be too narrow, indeed hopelessly inadequate, to account for corruption in the real world.

The approach heavily favoured by neo-liberal economics to conceptualize and model corruption in the public sector is what can be derived from traditional rent-seeking theory. Originating in a famous paper by Gordon Tulloch[4], the theory and the large literature it has generated over time have had a dominant influence on how most professional economists view corruption today.

The standard definition of rent-seeking is 'the quest for privileged benefits from government'[5]. In other words, the quest is to get a return without making a contribution; there are welfare and social costs attached to such economic behaviour. In this theoretical discourse, rent-seeking, which is problematic, must be clearly distinguished from profit-seeking, which is assumed to be beneficial to society. The 'first-best' scenario is the complete absence of rents of this kind. The 'second-best' is 'optimization' of its forms, welfare costs, and effects. In a well-known illustrative case taken up by rent-seeking theory, competitive lobbying and corruption are examined as two different forms of seeking preferential treatment by public decision-makers. What should policymakers do in this case? The answer is to focus on the resultant deviations from optimality and when this is done, corruption, being close to a 'pure transfer', turns out to be a less wasteful form of rent-seeking than competitive lobbying.

The diagnoses and the prescriptions veer towards

a narrow and predictable policy path. The problem is diagnosed as being the set of controls placed by the government upon economic activity in an otherwise free market. The prescription is to set the economy free from state control and let the market have free rein. Bardhan offers the critical insight that because 'the presumption often is that government is nothing but organised theft and the less of it the better'[6], much of the theory of rent-seeking does not worry about the fact that the objective is not only to reduce corruption in an official agency but also to avoid harm to 'the objective for which the agency was deployed in the first place'.

To be fair, there has been push-back by some economists studying corruption within the broad rent-seeking framework. The push-back, which focuses largely on identifying and estimating the welfare costs of different forms of rent-seeking and essentially argues that corruption is a significant obstacle to economic development and lowers welfare, attempts to pick some holes in the traditional theory without really undermining it.

It cannot be disputed that rent-seeking theory, with its latter-day modifications, yields some serviceable insights for the study of corruption in the public sector, although these insights largely revolve around the proposition that if there are controls, they are likely to be misused for corrupt purposes. The theory has the advantage of descriptive clarity and some internal consistency in its analysis, which compare favourably with much of the research done on corruption in political studies and by activists. However, the micro-economic theory is hopelessly inadequate as a conceptualization of the different types and forms of corruption. Aside from the fact that its more extreme iterations can be read as a justification for bribery, nepotism, and so forth, at least in comparison with more 'wasteful' forms of rent-seeking, it fails to see corruption as a 'configuration of corruption activities'[7] that make sense only when they are placed in historical, social, institutional, and, above all, political economy, context.

Just as corruption cannot be conceptualized in isolation from politics and society, its serving as a political economy mechanism for private aggrandizement in which the private sector and the state play closely aligned roles is crucial to understanding it in its various forms and manifestations. This is one reason the rent-seeking approach to corruption fails to explain why, far from fading away, corruption in its various forms has grown exponentially in the liberalization era in India. We will return to this issue in Chapter 6.

Corruption Through a Political Lens

A tractable definition most commonly used in political studies and by anti-corruption movements worldwide is the abuse of entrusted power for private gain. On the face of it, this is not very different from the standard definition economists use. However, this tractability is deceptive. For one thing, in its attempt at simplification, the definition misses out a great deal of the complexity, multifacetedness, and configurations of corruption in the real world. Secondly, by narrowing the idea of corruption so that it applies only to the public sector and to bribe-taking politicians and other public officials, it seriously underplays the supply side of corruption, that is, the active and often determinative role national and international business corporations, the private sector, and the black economy play in the exponential increase in corruption among politicians, bureaucrats, and intermediaries. Finally, the tractable definition runs into a mire of practical, that is, legal, criminological, and political, problems in most jurisdictions.

It is no wonder that the United Nations Convention Against Corruption (UNCAC), a potentially powerful global legal instrument that was adopted by the UN General Assembly in October 2003, and came into force in 2005, avoids definition. Instead, it lists and briefly describes specific types and forms of corruption: bribery, embezzlement, misappropriation, influence trading, money laundering, laundering the proceeds of crime, concealment, and obstruction of justice[8]. Subject to the fundamental principles of their legal systems, member states that are parties to the Convention commit themselves to preventing, and acting unwaveringly against, all these corruption offences. Further, they commit themselves to affording one another 'the widest measure of mutual assistance' in investigations, prosecutions, and judicial proceedings in relation to the offences covered by UNCAC.

Crucially, Article 12 of the UN Convention

requires countries to legislate and act effectively to 'prevent corruption involving the private sector, enhance accounting and auditing standards in the private sector and, where appropriate, provide effective, proportionate and dissuasive civil, administrative or criminal penalties to comply with such measures'. Article 16 calls for the adoption of legislative and other necessary measures to establish as a criminal offence the corruption of foreign public officials 'in order to obtain or retain business or other undue advantage in relation to the conduct of international business'.

The then UN Secretary General Kofi A. Annan's foreword to the published text of UNCAC delivered a fierce denunciation of corruption, which contrasted with the equivocal attitudes and apologetics found in some of the corruption literature in economics and other social sciences:

> Corruption is an insidious plague that has a wide range of corrosive effects on societies. It undermines democracy and the rule of law, leads to violations of human rights, distorts markets, erodes the quality of life and allows organised crime, terrorism and other threats to human security to flourish... This evil phenomenon is found in all countries—big and small, rich and poor—but it is in the developing world that its effects are most destructive. Corruption hurts the poor disproportionately... Corruption is a key element in economic underperformance

and a major obstacle to poverty alleviation and development.[9]

These are fine sentiments but as we will see in Chapter 6, using corruption as an explanatory variable for economic growth and performance is highly questionable.

India signed the Convention promptly in 2005 but dragged its feet for six years before ratifying it. And more than a decade after UNCAC entered into force, it is yet to put in place the necessary legislation and institutional arrangements and safeguards in compliance with Articles 12 and 16. In fact, India offers an instructive case study of how legal, criminological, and, above all, political economy factors thwart every attempt to get a firm handle on corruption with a view to preventing and rooting it out.

SIX

POLITICAL CORRUPTION THROUGH A MARXIST LENS

The Marxist understanding of political corruption foregrounds history, the history of the evolution of societies from one stage to another. It decisively rejects ahistorical theorizing about the forms and functions of corruption in society. It argues that 'corruption has always been an inherent feature of capitalism', not 'an aberration…a moral blight, an ethical lapse' in a rule-abiding society; and that it is prevalent in all types of capitalist societies, whether they are under bourgeois-democratic or authoritarian regimes or military dictatorships[1]. The Marxist understanding sees corruption as a problem of political economy and leaves no doubt about which class or classes are at the root of it.

It has been claimed that the founders of Marxism developed their revolutionary ideology without placing any emphasis on the corruption of the capitalist order they set out to supersede. But as one scholar points out, the writings of Marx and Lenin do show they were concerned about corruption within the socialist movement, with Lenin registering a great deal of concern and anxiety about the damaging effects of this corruption in his writings beginning late 1899. Both Marx and Lenin saw capitalist society as the source of corruption and while they 'did not reject capitalism because it was hopelessly corrupt', they believed that 'it could exert a corrupting influence on the movement which sought to transform bourgeois society'[2]. In several writings between late 1899 and 1917, Lenin expressed deep concern over the ways in which corruption in its multifariousness was being deployed with some success by the government, by capitalists, and by opportunists of various shades as a weapon to divide the working class, infect sections of it with the petty-bourgeois ideological outlook, and divert it from the class struggle. He firmly believed that a return to Marx's founding principles was necessary if the revolutionary movement was to be saved from corruption[3].

Peter Bratsis, an American Marxist political scientist, points out that with the rise of capitalism, a new notion of political corruption 'as being out of place' took shape and joined the age-old understanding of corruption as decay and destruction, shared by political thinkers from Aristotle to Machiavelli. He argues that this new understanding of corruption became 'the foundation of how capitalist societies were able to establish what constitutes normal and pathological presences of self-interests within the political sphere'. Only by differentiating between the normal and the pathological presences of private interests within political life can the fiction of some universal public interest be maintained. The 'omnipresence of private interests within the public' is thus legitimized, with some forms of this regarded as corruption and 'most presences of the private within the public...normalised'[4].

Central to the Marxist understanding of political corruption is the omnipresence of private interests—above all, the class interests behind big business, including multinationals—within the public sphere. Taking on the proposition underlying much of the current Indian discourse on corruption, that it is politicians and bureaucrats who are corrupt and that the 'few black sheep' among businessmen are created by the political and bureaucratic system, Prakash Karat, former general secretary of the Communist Party of India (Marxist), argues that:

> the fountainhead of corruption is big business and the neo-liberal policies… Increasingly, the political system is getting perverted by big capital. It is the illegal money generated by big business and the corporates which has corrupted the political system and not the other way around. The political system is getting moulded to accommodate the interests of a proliferating capitalism.[5]

Recent Marxist writings have touched upon the types and forms of corruption prevalent during different phases of the development of capitalist society, and in various countries with their distinctive economic systems and political cultures.

Against this historical background, it may be worth asking and pursuing the research question whether the specific forms of corruption and especially the grand corruption arrangements encountered in a developing country like India bear telltale signs of being engendered within a 'social formation', or amidst the interaction of coexisting and contending social formations (including their remnants and mutations), in the Marxist sense.

In *Capital*, Marx uses the term 'social formation' several times without defining it but Marxist scholars have tried to infer its rich meanings from the context as well as his varied and nuanced historical treatment of the concept in his magnum opus and in other writings. In *Reading Capital*, originally published in 1965, the French Marxist philosopher Louis Althusser conceptualizes a social formation as a structured complex of concrete economic, legal-political, and ideological relations 'belonging to a determinate mode of production'[6]. Elsewhere he characterizes historical materialism as 'the theory of the Marxist science of the development of social formations'[7]. Different social formations, or their historical remnants and mutations, can exist simultaneously within a country or a region or even a locality. They can be in contention and confrontation or they can coexist for quite a while, as the experience of modern India illustrates. Unevenness, variability, and mutability can be observed within a social formation. The relationship between particular forms of corruption and the social formation in which they exist can be taken up as a fruitful area of research.

A Paradigm Change

Bratsis calls attention to an important transformation that took place over the last two decades in the understanding of political corruption. Whereas it used to be viewed as essentially a domestic issue, it has now become

> one of the most central topics taken up by international organisations and actors... this international focus does not represent an abandonment of the ways that ideas and rules regarding corruption function to reproduce the social division of the public and the private. Rather, it signifies an addition to and further complication in how corruption is addressed. Corruption now, in addition to the earlier understandings...also comes to signify a lack of transparency.[8]

Contemporary Marxist writings on political corruption challenge the notion, promoted with great assiduity by transnational capital and various international organizations and actors, of 'corruption as opacity' and the consequent prescription of transparency as the antidote to corruption. They criticize the obsessive focus of international organizations on bureaucratic corruption at the expense of a serious effort to address corruption not as a pathological condition, but as an integral problem of political economy.

They reject any contraposition of high-level corruption with the everyday corruption encountered by ordinary citizens, suggesting instead that 'it is the institutionalised corruption at the top which creates and sustains the petty corruption at the lower levels'[9]. And they do not buy into the technocratic and moralistic fixes favoured by mainstream anti-corruption literature, arguing instead for a historical materialist approach to the question of political corruption today[10].

Marxists reject the neo-liberal ideological discourse of corruption as a cause of mass deprivation, inequality, and underdevelopment. In fact, they raise serious questions about using corruption as an explanatory variable for economic growth[11]. This they do on theoretical grounds and also on the basis of empirical data that show that countries like India and China that have had high levels of corruption have had high GDP growth rates. Some Marxist writers see in the international approaches to corruption a reiteration, at least in some respects, of the colonialist narrative on backwardness and corruption, namely that 'it is something within those people who are disadvantaged which can best explain their condition'[12].

Moving from theory to application, we can ask how the Marxist approaches make sense of one of the major developments in India's political economy over the past quarter century—the exponential increase and omnipresence of political corruption.

Corruption and Liberalization

Those whose standard argument used to be that India's 'permit-licence-quota raj' was the raison d'être of corruption and that deregulation and liberalization would lead to its prevention and elimination have a lot of explaining to do on why the dismantling of that raj has ushered in corruption in a much greater variety of forms and on an unimaginably vaster scale. The essential answer they offer is that many vestiges of the licence raj remain, enforcement capacity is weak, and the reform process needs to be given more time to bring down the level of rent-seeking. This is the equivalent of a faith healer's approach to a serious disease.

Bardhan, who occupies ground somewhere between rent-seeking theory and radical approaches to corruption, has a more sophisticated explanation. The key structural reasons for the exponential growth of corruption in recent years are the shooting up, as a consequence of higher economic growth, of the market value of scarce public resources such as land, oil and gas fields, mineral resources, and the telecommunication spectrum and the enhanced opportunities for making money from their favoured allocation by a public authority; more expensive elections; major policy changes involving large-scale transfers of funds from the central and state governments to local-level bodies; and the social churning resulting from 'the rise of hitherto subordinate social groups in political power'[13].

In a recently published study of caste, class, and capital

in the making of economic policy across Indian states, Kanta Murali[14] touches on the issue of corruption and its relation to the variable pro-business strategies of Indian states. Noting that 'growth strategies in the aftermath of neoliberalism typically require that policy makers privilege capital over other sections of society, at least in the short term', she proposes that pro-business strategies and crony capitalism[15] can be thought of as lying on a continuum:

> The degree of arbitrariness and discretion in the state's policy measures increases as we move from pro-business frameworks to crony capitalist ones. The former benefits a larger section of capitalists while the latter privileges a smaller, select group within the business community who have strong political connections. While corruption can exist in pro-business policy frameworks, it typically does so and is more extensive under crony capitalism. But it is important to note that crony capitalism and corruption can co-exist with growth. The sheer number of corruption scandals in India in its period of high growth offers clear evidence of this.

In Karat's analysis, in the pre-liberalization era the source of corruption at high levels was big business bribing ministers and officials to seek favours either for licences or for bypassing certain regulations. But with liberalization and deregulation, 'the entire policy...is put up for sale', with foreign and Indian big business interests 'free to make the highest bid for policies for an entire industry' such as telecommunications, power, and oil. Further, these policies can be changed overnight, for the right price. 'Under the neo-liberal regime,' Karat concludes, 'the state becomes the handmaiden and the facilitator of the transfer of the resources of the country to big business. Scarce resources are cornered by the big corporates, big contractors, and real estate promoters with the help of the government'[16]. The Marxist economist C. P. Chandrasekhar approaches the same question from a somewhat different angle:

> In all societies, there are scarcities of one kind or another: access to the best free hospital facilities; access to land; access to a scarce 'intangible' resource like the air waves; or rights to extract limited and non-reproducible mineral resources, to name just a few. In a regulated regime, there are well-defined rules on how this is to be done. Those rules can be violated, but there are well-defined procedures and benchmarks to decide whether unwarranted access has been provided to one or other agent. In a liberalised economic order, on the other hand, while the government still has the right to determine the level of access, its role is seen as one of providing such access as part of a process of encouraging private sector-led growth... The essential point is that corruption tends to be greater in periods when there is a state-engineered redistribution of wealth in favour of a few and at the explicit or implicit expense of the many. Liberalisation is one such period...[17]

This insight can go some way, but only some way, towards answering a difficult question confronting Marxists: why does China, a socialist country with its 'socialist market economy', have such high levels of corruption, making President and Party General Secretary Xi Jinping take up the anti-corruption drive against 'tigers and flies'—powerful leaders as well as low-ranking cadres—as one of his top political projects?

What this chapter suggests is that even if Marxists cannot claim to have all the answers to the question of corruption and its forms and functions in political economy[18], theorists and moral crusaders who come from other positions can learn from the theoretical perspectives and lived experience that Marxism brings to the subject. For those who do not approach the larger questions of political economy it raises with ideological blinkers, these insights can help make better sense of the state of corruption in India today.

SECTION III

TWO CASE STUDIES

SEVEN

BOFORS: THE DEFINING GRAND CORRUPTION SCANDAL

A corrupt state of things is very frequently represented as an 'abuse'; it is taken for granted that the foundation was good—the system, the institution itself is faultless—but that…the arbitrary volition of men has made use of that which in itself was good to further its own selfish ends, and that all that is required to be done is to remove these adventitious elements. On this showing the institute in question escapes obloquy, and the evil that disfigures it appears something foreign to it… A great and general corruption…is quite another thing.

—Georg Wilhelm Friedrich Hegel,
The Philosophy of History, 1820s

I came upon grand corruption in the flesh during *The Hindu*'s protracted investigation of the Bofors howitzer deal scandal in the late 1980s. The origins of the term, which is now widely used in international anti-corruption discourse, go back to Hegel's famous characterization of the state of the pre-Reformation Catholic Church as 'a great and general corruption'.

Bofors, as I have already noted, is independent India's defining grand corruption scandal. Given the complexities of Indian politics, its political and social impact is extremely hard to measure, but there can be little doubt that it contributed significantly to the downfall of Rajiv Gandhi's Congress party in the November 1989 Lok Sabha election.

A 16 April 1987 broadcast by a reporter, Magnus Nilsson, on *Dagens Eko*, the news arm of Swedish public radio, had started it all:

> At Bofors, the work with the big Indian order began already in the late 1970s and from then on till the contract was signed in March last year the company was aided by an Indian agent who helped Bofors with local contacts and support within the Indian military authorities, within the bureaucracy, and within Prime Minister [Rajiv] Gandhi's Congress Party. In November last year Bofors began paying remunerations to the Indian contacts who had helped the company, but the money was not directly sent to India. Instead it was sent to secret bank accounts in Suisse Bank in Geneva...[1]

The *Dagens Eko* news broadcast, which was relayed by international news agencies, went on to specify that three payments totalling 29.5 million Swedish kroner were made in mid-November 1986 and a fourth payment of 2.5 million kroner was made in December. Mentioning that the code name for the transactions was 'Lotus' and that these 1986 payments were 'only part of the total remuneration to the Indian contacts', the broadcast quoted unnamed sources within Bofors AB as saying that the company would end up paying 'commission...of a couple of hundred million kroner in all...in connection with the Indian deal'. Nilsson concluded his broadcast on a sharp-edged note that sent shock waves through political India:

> How large a part of this money is remuneration for the Indian agent's work for Bofors and how much simply is pure bribes is uncertain, but that the main part of this money has been passed on as pure bribes is confirmed by persons with very clear insight into how the deal between Bofors and India was handled.

The broad denials issued by the Indian government and the studied denials, which on scrutiny turned out to be non-denials, put out by Bofors AB carried no credibility, especially in India. A week after the *Dagens Eko* broadcast, *Dagens Nyheter* published two reports alleging that the Hindujas had received a commission from the company. While G. P. Hinduja dismissed the reports as totally untrue, the Bofors statement that no money had been paid to the Hindujas 'to win the contract' appeared to contradict him, by implying that money had been paid for something else, which was anyone's guess at that point[2].

It is not clear why, after this promising start, the Swedish news media went low-key, if not virtually silent, on the payoffs in the Bofors-India howitzer deal. But whatever be the explanation, we in *The Hindu* knew that a window had opened for us. From now on, it would have to be the Indian press in determined, dogged, and, where required, aggressive pursuit of the truth behind the secret payments into the Swiss bank accounts that Nilsson had originally reported.

Along with the *Indian Express*, then edited by Arun Shourie, we were quick off the mark, sensing a rare investigative journalistic opportunity given the context—social-democratic Sweden's much-vaunted commitment to transparency and its reputation for not being able to hide anything for too long, and the highly favourable socio-political climate created in India by V. P. Singh's revolt. But for months it seemed we were in a frustrating race to get to the truth, with little to show for our exertions.

When we cast about, in India and in Europe, for relevant information and background on the howitzer deal and the alleged payoffs, we knew that corruption, influence-peddling, and various forms of law-breaking were pervasive in the international arms trade. The challenge was to break through the walls of secrecy that had been fortified all around following some embarrassing whistle-blower leaks. We had a general idea that arms exports by Swedish companies violating the law or circumventing the prohibitions on weapons sales to belligerents, and corrupt deals involving bribes and kickbacks concealed as 'commissions' to middlemen and foreign officials were becoming a hot topic in Sweden. But in the pre-Internet era and given the fact that most of the relevant material was in Swedish, we had very little information on the specifics of these unsavoury business transactions.

A recently declassified CIA paper, dated 4 March 1988, on 'Sweden's Bofors Arms Scandal'[3] fills in the necessary background, which would have been helpful in providing perspective and context to our investigation into the Bofors-India howitzer deal had we had access to this information at the time. The transactions mentioned in the sanitized document include Bofors AB's sale of more than 300 RBS-70 missile systems to Bahrain and Dubai via Singapore in 1979; its sale of twenty-two anti-aircraft guns to Thailand via Singapore in 1985; its sale of ammunition to Oman via Italy; its alleged sale of RBS-70 missile systems to Iran via Singapore; its alleged bribing of Indian middlemen and officials in connection with India's $1.5 billion purchase of 155mm howitzers; its alleged bribery of an official in Singapore in connection with arms sales to other countries; its alleged sale of naval ordnance to Taiwan; its alleged sale of explosives to the German Democratic Republic via Austria; Nobel Kemi AB's sale of 2,139 metric tonnes of munitions to Iran, Iraq, Syria, Egypt, and Burma via Austria, the GDR, Italy, and Yugoslavia, with about two-thirds of these munitions going to Iran; and Karl-Erik Schmitz, a private Swedish businessman, acting as an international broker for arms sales, including sales of weapons produced by Sweden, to proscribed countries.

The document lists the various investigations, enquiries, reviews, and prosecutions launched in these cases. It notes that in January 1987, Carl-Fredrik Algernon, Inspector General of Military Equipment, was found dead under distressing circumstances in Stockholm half an hour after meeting Anders Carlberg, head of Bofors AB's parent company, Nobel Industries; Algernon had been 'struck by a subway train' in a probable case of suicide.

'Swedish arms manufacturers experiencing financial difficulties in the late 1970s and early 1980s', the CIA paper observes, 'determined they needed to sell arms to proscribed countries in order to remain financially viable. Government officials acquiesced… The lingering Bofors AB and Nobel Kemi AB arms scandals, which first came to light in 1984, owe to the failure of Sweden's private and public sector leaders to observe their own rules governing arms exports in an apparent effort to bolster the domestic arms industry… Numerous investigations were initiated to examine the complex web of bribery and arms diversions but, despite an admission from a key industry executive only two individuals have been charged with violating Swedish law: a Nobel Kemi manager and a private arms trader'.

India was not a proscribed country for Swedish arms sales. But it was clear that for political reasons the Social Democratic government of Ingvar Carlsson was intent on damage limitation and cover-up in the howitzer deal; and most opposition politicians, for their own reasons, closed ranks behind the government. The official investigation into the alleged Bofors bribes to Indian officials was quickly called off. Even before Nilsson's explosive broadcast, Martin Ardbo, the managing director of Bofors AB between 1982 and 1987, had lost his job for transgressions unrelated to India. Subsequently, in December 1989, he and some other former Bofors executives were found guilty of serious offences, including 'gross smuggling', but got away lightly, escaping prison as well as fines[4].

When strenuous damage limitation and cover-up efforts were under way in India and Sweden, a tip came to us from unexpected quarters. During the course of an informal conversation at the Rashtrapati Bhavan in 1988, R. Venkataraman, President of India who had held various key ministerial portfolios, including defence, and was known for his integrity, said to me, 'Don't you know that the standard rate of commission in major defence deals is 6 per cent?' This was valuable background information, given the authoritative source. We knew by then that the percentage-based kickbacks, disguised as commissions, that Bofors AB was contracted to pay for winning the India howitzer deal considerably exceeded this standard rate.

As the separate investigations by *The Hindu* and the *Indian Express* progressed, gathering pace but taking different directions, we realized two things. Competitive pressure, instead of putting us at risk of cutting corners, had the effect of focusing our investigative efforts, pushing us to verify and verify again every detail we learnt. It also helped us understand that competing newspapers and journalists could cooperate with, and reinforce and reassure, each other in certain areas of the investigation.

Behind *The Hindu*'s Investigation

The Hindu's investigation was not the work of any one star journalist but a collective enterprise, which I happened to lead and do much of the writing for; and for more than eighteen months from April 1988, when *The Hindu*'s Geneva stringer, Chitra Subramaniam, struck gold in Stockholm, until October 1989, when we published the withheld secret part of the Swedish National Audit Bureau's findings, *The Hindu* owned the investigation—thanks to its exclusive continuing relationship with the confidential source Chitra had found and had persuaded to cooperate with us.

A quarter century after *The Hindu* got lucky in Stockholm, our confidential source, who had long retired by then, went on record to reveal that he was Sten Lindstrom, an experienced police officer with strong views on right and wrong[5]. As head of the investigation department of the Swedish National Bureau of Investigation (NBI), he had personally investigated the Bofors-India payoffs and had had all the incriminating papers seized. He described this discovery as an 'accident':

> We were conducting several search and seize operations in the premises of Bofors and their executives. I have some experience in this area, so I asked my team to take everything they could find. In the pile were one set of documents to Swiss banks with instructions that the name of the recipient should be blocked out. An accountant doing his job asked why anonymity was necessary since the payments were legal. Bofors was unable to explain and then we found more and more documents leading to India.[6]

Lindstrom was our principal and key source through the investigation. He explained that he had leaked the Bofors-India documents to *The Hindu* because, as a Swedish citizen 'raised in the best traditions of social-democracy', he had been morally outraged and shocked by 'the scale of political involvement in Sweden breaking all rules including those we set for ourselves'[7]. During our interaction on Bofors, he asked for nothing more than fair, accurate, and contextualized use of the material he was providing and I can confirm that no material benefits or rewards of any kind were asked for or given. The investigation was hugely dependent on the photocopies of the documents he was passing on to us. However, our confidential source was not willing to part with everything he had in one go. He would leak the documents only in phased instalments over a period of eighteen months, so it was a process of negotiating with him for more and waiting patiently for the next lot. But he was good enough to give us a general idea of what was to come in the next round.

At our newspaper's headquarters in Chennai, we were sensitive to our confidential source's position and the personal risks he was taking. At one point, we sensed that the Indian government had surmised, perhaps even arrived at the conclusion through a process of elimination, that Lindstrom was the leaker. But we knew that the government could not go public with its suspicions for a simple reason: publicly naming the head of the investigation, the senior police officer who had ordered the incriminating documents to be seized, as the leaker would only add to its woes by authenticating the documents leaked in the eyes of the public. We were deeply concerned when we heard that a complaint had been made about the leaks and an enquiry was being conducted by the Swedish authorities against our confidential source; and we were relieved when the enquiry apparently found no evidence of wrongdoing.

But Lindstrom was not our only source. During our long-drawn-out investigation, we met and talked with the Hinduja brothers, two of whom had figured in the documents leaked to *The Hindu*. We talked to Win Chadha, the original Bofors agent mentioned by Nilsson in the *Dagens Eko* broadcast; he had called me long distance to protest his innocence and to pressure us to call off the hunt. We talked to Myles Stott, a fiduciary who handled the financial affairs of A. E. Services Limited, a shell company to which Bofors AB had made a $7.34 million payoff in September 1986. We searched the companies registry in the UK for information and clues relating to the shell companies and their directors. We talked to various sources about the business dealings of Ottavio Quattrocchi, the 'Q' of the Ardbo diary who had close relations with the Rajiv Gandhi family; it turned out that the Snamprogetti representative in India was the mover behind the Bofors payments to A. E. Services Limited. We also talked to confidential political sources within the Joint Parliamentary Committee (JPC) who had been given access to a mass of official documentation related to the decision-making on the choice of howitzer and confidential talks with Bofors representatives; one JPC member, Aladi Aruna of the All India Anna Dravida Munnetra Kazhagam (AIADMK), who had turned hostile to the government, his party's ally, and had attached a note of dissent to the JPC's cover-up report, gave us invaluable information that led to an investigative breakthrough. We interviewed Swedish Prime Minister Carlsson on what he knew about the Bofors payoffs and why his government was not doing more to get at the truth. During the eighteen months when *The Hindu* owned the investigation, I had confidential one-on-one meetings on Bofors with CBI Director Mohan Katre, Defence Minister K. C. Pant, Arun Nehru, who had once been close to Rajiv Gandhi but had turned against him, officials in the Prime Minister's Office, and, finally, Prime Minister Rajiv Gandhi himself, all at their request. I must add that during this period a few other publications in Sweden and India, notably *India Today*, contributed some new information and insights that helped fill in some gaps and make better sense of a complex story.

Know Your Bofors

The Bofors scandal revolved around the Rajiv Gandhi government's decision to purchase from the Swedish arms manufacturing company an advanced 155mm howitzer system. The transaction was valued at SEK 8.41 billion (₹1,437.72 crore or $1.4 billion at the prevailing exchange rate). It turned out that unacknowledged payments aggregating ₹64 crore or US$ 50 million—termed 'commissions' and calculated on a *percentage* basis—had been paid by Bofors into secret Swiss bank accounts *after* the contract was won on 24 March 1986.

The payoffs were in violation of the formal assurances sought and obtained from Bofors by the Government of India. The evidentiary basis for the investigation was the documentation leaked to *The Hindu* by the confidential source, the key documents being the Swiss bank papers, transaction documents, secret contracts, and a diary and notes kept by Ardbo, which had been seized by the Swedish police.

What we learnt early on in our investigation was that the documents in hand or in the pipeline were vital to the story, but the story should not get lost in the web of complexity that surrounded the transactions. There were also false trails, leading to persons who were in no way involved in the scandal. For example, a leading lawyer, going by unrelated events and misleading proximities, wrongly accused Amitabh Bachchan of involvement in Bofors and this was prominently reported in a section of the press. But our investigation showed that this was completely baseless and we had no hesitation in making this clear.

But above all, we learnt that making sense of the documents, fitting them in a larger frame that was slowly taking shape, was what the Bofors investigation was about. No journalistic investigation would be complete and there would always be gaps to be filled that we could not fill.

Let me digress here on the role of documents in investigation. It is true that documents are often the best evidence and, for the informed public, they can be clinching proof of corruption or abuse of power or other wrongdoing. The massive troves of confidential, secret, and hidden documents released, over the past decade, by WikiLeaks, and the game-changing documented disclosures by Edward Snowden on global surveillance by the US National Security Agency underline this point. However, this caution issued against document fetishism by Kim Philby, one of modern history's great practitioners of ideologically inspired espionage, must be heeded: 'Just because a document is a document, it has a glamour which tempts the reader to give it more weight than it deserves...documentary intelligence, to be really valuable, must come in a steady stream, embellished with an awful lot of explanatory annotation. An hour's serious discussion with a trustworthy informant is often more valuable than any number of original documents. Of course, it is best to have both.'[8]

As more and more details, documented and otherwise, emerged in our investigation, we needed to zoom out to get a historical perspective, and then the Bofors-India corruption story seemed to come alive. Now it could be understood in terms of five modes of action. The first was the decision-making on the choice of howitzer and the motive for the crime clearly lay here. The second mode comprised the arrangements for the payoffs. The third was the cover-up and crisis management. The fourth was the journalistic investigation and exposé. The fifth was the CBI's long-delayed, on-and-off criminal investigation, assisted by the Swiss Federal Police and the Swiss courts, and prosecution before Judge Ajit Bharihoke's Special Court for CBI cases.

What was the hard information we had on decision-making on the howitzer? The official and commercial documents in hand revealed that from 1980 the Government of India was looking out for a state-of-the-art 155mm howitzer system to meet defence operational requirements that were said to be urgent. The competition was shortlisted in December 1982 to M/s Sofma of France, M/s AB Bofors of Sweden, M/s International Military Services of the United Kingdom, and M/s Voest Alpine of Austria. In November 1985, the Government of India's choice, based on advice from Army Headquarters and a recommendation by the Negotiating Committee, narrowed down to Sofma and Bofors.

The official record also showed that between October 1982 and February 1986, the Indian Army carried out no fewer than seven evaluations of the relative merits of the howitzer systems offered by the shortlisted bidders. General A. S. Vaidya was army chief for most of this period, from 31 July 1983 to 31 January 1986. In the first six evaluations, the Sofma 155mm TR howitzer, with its extended range, was decisively preferred to the Bofors gun. Financial considerations also gave the French manufacturer what seemed to be an unbeatable lead. However, Prime Minister Rajiv Gandhi and a small group of ministers and officials who knew his thinking had made up their minds to award the contract to the Swedish arms manufacturer. Since they knew no way to make army headquarters under General Vaidya budge from its preference for the French gun, they patiently waited it out, notwithstanding the urgency of the strategic military requirements.

When General Vaidya's retirement neared and even before General K. Sundarji formally took over as army chief, the Prime Minister and his confidants moved swiftly to clinch the deal they wanted. With army headquarters reversing in February 1986 a succession of professional judgements that had gone against Bofors, the stages of final decision-making were telescoped and rushed through, resulting in the formalization of the choice of Bofors on 24 March 1986. Subsequently, the CBI charge sheet revealed that after the Negotiating Committee recommended, on

12 March, that a Letter of Intent be issued to Bofors, the file was approved by five officials and three ministers on a single day, 13 March, and was finally approved by Rajiv Gandhi on 14 March.

The decision-making mode could now be related to the payments mode, that is, the contracted arrangements for secret payments into the Swiss bank accounts. We could see that these two modes constituted a cohesive set, belonging to the past, and the government could do nothing about this. The other three modes of action—the cover-up and crisis management, the journalistic investigation, and the CBI's criminal investigation and prosecution, which were all continuing—constituted another, less cohesive set.

It can be seen from this that investigative journalism is not just about technique, documentation, and data analysis, although these are essential requirements for a complex investigation. They must be consciously understood to be a means to an end, a coherent, nuanced, compelling story that would make sense to an informed public, raise awareness of the main issues, perhaps serve as a catalyst for progressive change or reform, and fully justify the time, effort, and resources invested in the investigation.

'But what good came of it at last?'[9]

Little Peterkin's meaningful question to Old Kaspar in Robert Southey's anti-war poem is worth asking about the investigation into the Bofors corruption scandal.

The answer must necessarily be complex, nuanced, and inconclusive. There is little doubt that Bofors and *The Hindu*'s investigation and exposé, which was triggered by the *Dagens Eko* broadcast of 16 April 1987, made a big political impact, the kind of impact that no single corruption case has made in India before and after Bofors. Investigative journalism played the lead role in bringing the truth to light but it would be a mistake to think that the impact was the contribution of journalism alone. It was the political opposition spearheaded by V. P. Singh that took the work of journalism far and wide, deep into society and the polity, and developed it into a major election campaign theme.

Let me digress a little here on investigative journalism and the question of impact. Every journalist working determinedly to unearth the truth desires impact. The success of investigative journalism is often judged by whether it is able to generate change in the desired direction. But there are obvious problems with applying this criterion. For one thing, it exaggerates the role the news media play, assigning to them a power to shape the larger external environment that they clearly do not have. Secondly, the impact of journalism on complex socio-economic and political realities is extremely hard to measure. Even in the case of the most celebrated journalistic investigation of the last fifty years, Watergate, the jury is still out on whether it made any real difference to politics in the United States and it would be an exaggeration to say that 'it brought down a President'.

One part of the answer to little Peterkin's question, as it applies to Bofors, is that what prevailed at the bar of public opinion and politics failed and eventually collapsed at the bar of public prosecution. The cover-up strategy adopted by the Indian and Swedish governments between 1987 and 1989 meant that the investigators faced an uphill task after a criminal case was registered by the CBI in January 1990, nearly three years after *Dagens Eko* broadcast the allegations. Evidence that could have been collected from Bofors AB and the Swedish investigators had a case been registered by an independent-minded CBI in April 1987, or at least after *The Hindu* published the first set of documents in April 1988, was irremediably lost. Moreover, the cover-up and damage limitation efforts were resumed when the Congress, headed by P.V. Narasimha Rao, formed a minority government in 1991, and once again after a rejuvenated Congress returned to power at the head of a new coalition, the United Progressive Alliance, in 2004.

As the Bofors corruption case slowly made its way through the courts and the administrative-bureaucratic processes in India and Switzerland, the main accused, Rajiv Gandhi, was assassinated (on 21 May 1991, halfway through the 10th Lok Sabha election). A decade later, two other key accused, S. K. Bhatnagar, who had been defence secretary at the time of the conclusion of the Bofors howitzer deal, and Win Chadha, the Bofors agent, were dead. In July 1993, the Swiss federal court ruled that India was entitled to receive Swiss bank documents relevant to the case. Two weeks later, Quattrocchi, who was deeply implicated in the scandal, was allowed by the Narasimha Rao government to flee India, never to return. In January 1997, Swiss bank documents running to more than 500 pages were released to India. In February 1997, after the CBI had formed a special investigation team for the case, letters rogatory were sent to Malaysia and the United Arab Emirates seeking the arrest of Quattrocchi and Chadha. In July 1999, during the Kargil conflict with Pakistan a decade after the V. P. Singh government had barred Bofors from entering into any defence contract with India, the BJP-led National Democratic Alliance government reversed the decision on national security grounds. By all accounts the 155mm Bofors howitzer performed effectively in the conflict.

On 22 October 1999, the CBI filed the first charge sheet in the case against Chadha, Quattrocchi, Bhatnagar, Ardbo and Bofors AB; Rajiv Gandhi figured in the charge sheet as 'an accused not sent for trial' because the case against him had abated with his death. Thereafter, the trial court issued arrest warrants against Quattrocchi and summons to the four other accused. With the CBI failing in its efforts to have the Italian businessman extradited from Malaysia, and with Ardbo out of the law's reach, only Chadha, who returned to India in March 2000, and Bhatnagar, who was ill with terminal cancer, seemed to be candidates for trial at this point. Then in October 2000, the CBI filed a supplementary charge sheet against S. P. Hinduja, G. P. Hinduja, and P. P. Hinduja; and in November 2002, the trial court ordered the framing of charges in the Bofors payoff case against the three brothers, after rejecting their plea for discharge from the case. In July 2003, the UK acceded to India's request to freeze Quattrocchi's bank accounts; and in January 2004, the Swiss authorities agreed to consider the CBI's request for providing Quattrocchi's bank details. It seemed that there was going to be a breakthrough in the legal case nearly seventeen years after the allegations of corruption had first surfaced. But this was not to be and a series of judicial and political reverses followed.

Out of the blue, on 4 February 2004, the Delhi High Court quashed the charges under the Prevention of Corruption Act against the three Hinduja brothers, holding that there was no evidence whatsoever to support the allegation that they had bribed Prime Minister Gandhi or Defence Secretary Bhatnagar for winning the Bofors howitzer contract. With this blow, the Bofors corruption case was virtually dead, although the court upheld the trial court's decision to frame charges of cheating and corruption against the three Hinduja brothers and also to frame charges of fabrication of documents against Bofors AB. These excerpts from Justice J. D. Kapoor's 115-page order are instructive: they show how unpredictable the Indian judiciary can be when it comes to assessing evidence and applying the rules of evidence to a case:

> The facts of the case itself show that so far as the public servants—Rajiv Gandhi and S. K. Bhatnagar—are concerned, 16 years of investigation by a premier

agency of the country—the Central Bureau of Investigation—could not unearth a scintilla of evidence against them for having accepted bribe/ illegal gratification in awarding the contract in favour of A. B. Bofors... All efforts by the CBI ended in a fiasco as they could not lay hand upon any secret or known account of these public servants where the alleged money might have found its abode either in Swiss banks or any other bank or vault. Charges for the offences punishable under Sections 120B (criminal conspiracy) of the Indian Penal Code (IPC) and Section 5 (2) read with Section 5 (1) (d) of the Prevention of Corruption Act, 1947, and Section 165A (public servant obtaining valuable thing, without consideration, from a person concerned in any proceeding or business transacted by such public servant) read with 161 (accepting gratification other than legal remuneration) against the petitioners for having entered into a criminal conspiracy with the public servants to cheat the Government of India and having abetted the public servants to commit criminal conduct by abusing their official position and taken illegal gratification for awarding the contract are quashed.[10]

The final judicial blow came on 31 May 2005 when the Delhi High Court cleared the three Hinduja brothers as well as Bofors AB of the remaining charges framed under the 4 February 2004 order of the High Court. Justice

R. S. Sodhi's order quashing the charges was essentially on the ground that the CBI could not satisfy the court that the copies of the documents it had produced to substantiate the charges, including the documents it had obtained from me, were admissible as evidence under the Evidence Act. Like Justice Kapoor, Justice Sodhi could not resist the temptation to chastise the CBI but he went further and registered sympathy for the accused, whom he evidently regarded as innocent victims:

> Before parting, I must express my disapproval at the investigation that went on for 14 years and I was given to understand that it cost the Exchequer nearly rupees 250 crores. During the investigation a huge bubble was created with the aid of the media which, however, when tested by court, burst leaving behind a disastrous trail of suffering. The accused suffered emotionally. Careers—both political and professional—were ruined besides causing huge economic loss. Many an accused lived and died with a stigma. It is hoped that this elite Investigating Agency will be more responsible in future.[11]

After these deadly blows, what remained were the formalities of burying l'affaire Bofors. On 31 December 2005, the CBI informed the UK's Crown Prosecution Service that it had not been able to link the money in Quattrocchi's two UK accounts with the Bofors payments; and a week later the accounts were unfrozen. In February 2007, the Italian businessman was detained at Argentina's

Iguazu international airport on an Interpol red corner notice and sent to custody. But the CBI under the UPA government was not going to extend itself to get the Italian businessman extradited even if that were possible. It failed to produce the necessary legal documents in court, lost the case, and subsequently withdrew all charges against him. With Quattrocchi's death from a stroke in July 2013, the Bofors corruption case reached its natural end.

But the epitaph had been written in advance, by chief metropolitan magistrate Vinod Yadav, while discharging Quattrocchi in 2011. The CBI, despite 'spending through the nose for about 21 years,' he observed, 'has not been able to put forward legally sustainable evidence with regard to conspiracy in the matter. Further, in the case of Mr. Quattrocchi, as against the alleged kickback of Rs. 64 crore he received, the CBI had by 2005 already spent around Rs. 250 crore on the investigation, which is sheer wastage of public money'. The magistrate then went on to quote two famous lines from an old Hindi film song—'Woh afsana jisse anjaam tak laana na ho mumkin, usse ek khoobsurat mod dekhar chhodna hi achha' (A story that cannot be taken to a logical end, it is better to leave it at a good juncture)[12].

The moral of the story could well be that the 'good juncture' had been reached in October 1989, when the journalistic investigation had done virtually all it could, proved its case in the court of public opinion, and made a worthwhile difference to politics by bringing the issue of grand corruption to the fore. And that was that.

EIGHT

TAMIL NADU'S SCIENTIFIC SYSTEM OF POLITICAL CORRUPTION

Basing ourselves on newspaper reports, we can reasonably hypothesize that there are distinctive corruption systems in several Indian states, with well-established patterns, expertly formulated and enforced rules of the game, identifiable actors, and regional and local specificities.

One of the most notorious and deadly corruption systems of long standing in a major state is BJP-ruled Madhya Pradesh's 'Vyapam', named after the Vyavsayik Pariksha Mandal or the Professional Examination Board (PEB), a self-financing and autonomous state body that conducts standardized tests for admission to various professional courses and for thousands of government jobs. PEB claims on its website that as the only set-up of its kind in India, it conducts sensitive examinations 'with complete impartiality and transparency, maintaining a very high standard of confidentiality'[1]. Even if we assume that it has cleaned up its act, more or less, its track record reveals that the claim is perverse.

Vyapam, which went on for many years but came to light only in 2013, is much more than a scam or even a mega-scam. It is grand corruption in the full-blown sense: a politically sanctioned and policy-enabled system of racketeering that has extracted bribes and kickbacks running into hundreds of crores of rupees in exchange for fixing the results of supposedly competitive tests for admission to state-run medical colleges and for thousands of government jobs. Vyapam involves a set of ingeniously devised criminal services provided, on a rate-card basis, by the racketeers to students and job-seekers to cheat their way into state-run medical colleges and government jobs. Vyapam is a deadly criminal enterprise, involving blackmail, intimidation, and violence, and resulting in the 'unnatural deaths' of several suspects, accused persons, and victims[2]. Vyapam is an example of the systematic subversion of a state's administration and, even more damagingly, its system of medical education and medical practice. Vyapam is the cynical exploitation of a situation of high unemployment and the desperate search for jobs. It has brought suffering, hardship, anxiety, and demoralization to large numbers of young men and women seeking educational opportunity and advancement, and ensnared into crooked ways by the racketeers.

When you look deeper, Vyapam turns out to be more than large-scale racketeering and grand corruption. It is, as Aman Sethi, a discerning journalist, puts it, 'a vast societal swindle—one that reveals the hollowness at the heart of practically every Indian state institution: inadequate schools, a crushing shortage of meaningful jobs, a corrupt government, a cynical middle class happy to cheat the system to aid their own children, a compromised and inept police force and a judiciary incapable of enforcing its laws'[3].

But this is not all. Vyapam is also contagion. The modus developed and perfected over the years in this sordid and deadly racket has spawned another admission racket, the Dental and Medical Test (DMAT) conducted by the Association of Private Dental and Medical Colleges of Madhya Pradesh for admission to the private medical and dental colleges in the state. Described by the news media as a 'high-end scam'[4], as worse than Vyapam by the Supreme Court of India[5], and as many times bigger than the PEB scam by the CBI[6], which however pleaded that it did not have the manpower to take this on, the DMAT racket has from its inception in 2006 boasted a star cast of beneficiaries. They include BJP and Congress political leaders, bureaucrats and police officials, and judges. The DMAT scandal has been estimated by Anand Rai, an RTI activist and whistle-blower, to have netted the scamsters anything between ₹8,000 crore and ₹10,000 crore[7].

Politically, Vyapam implicates or features senior BJP and RSS leaders, including ministers, in addition to a vast array of bureaucrats, intermediaries, fixers, and the participant victims, many hundreds of students and job-seekers ensnared in the racket. What is more, allegations have been made by the Congress against Shivraj Singh Chouhan, a three-term BJP chief minister, of involvement in the scandal and, at the very least, in its attempted cover-up. The political fight-back by the opposition, extensive recent coverage in the news media, and public-spirited litigation in the higher courts have obliged the BJP government to agree to bring in the CBI, resulting in a Supreme Court order transferring the investigation of Vyapam as well as the deaths allegedly related to it to the premier criminal investigating agency. While there is no certainty about how long the CBI's investigation will take and where it will lead, it is politically significant that Vyapam has unravelled at a time when the party ruling at the centre has attempted to seize the moral high ground, painting its political opponents as incorrigibly corrupt and making out that its own ideology and programme of 'Hindutva' are the very antithesis of corruption in an all-embracing sense.

One of the unexplained things about Vyapam is how it could have been covered up for so long, considering that it reached deep into society and involved the lives and livelihood of many thousands of people. The news media, especially the thriving Hindi language press, must accept their share of the responsibility for not bringing this vast societal swindle, which had calamitous consequences, to light earlier.

What this also suggests is that while there has been useful empirical research on different forms of corruption prevailing across the land, inadequate attention has been paid by scholars to state- or region-specific systems of political corruption that have been developed over time by national as well as regional parties, and in some notable cases by strong and charismatic political leaders. This academic deficit can be observed in the empirical as well as theoretical literature. There is a need to fill this knowledge gap by undertaking focused research, empirical as well as theoretical, into these systems so that a composite picture of the unevenness and diversity as well as the maturation of corruption arrangements across politically federal India can be built up, with implications for how to combat them.

To make a start towards filling this knowledge gap, this chapter presents a sketch for a study of Tamil Nadu's signature corruption system, the software for which has been repeatedly updated and upgraded, and aggressively protected over the past three-and-a-half decades. Like some ingeniously deep-seated and virulent malware, the OS—the system software that manages the hardware and software resources and provides common services for the state-wide corruption activities—has proved to be virtually ineradicable.

This is a textbook case of grand corruption that operates year-round with clockwork, 'scientific' precision. It has specified rates for *facilitative*, *collusive*, and *extractive* corruption[8], depending on the sector; fixed collection quotas, sweetened with incentives, for ministers, bureaucrats, and other collection agents; and no-nonsense enforcement of the rules. As with the best clockwork, smooth running and noiselessness are at a premium. This corruption system protects itself by instituting tens of criminal defamation and even sedition cases against media organizations, journalists, politicians, and anyone else who dares to criticize or attack the chief minister or the government—and not just on issues of corruption and abuse of power. With magistrates generally taking the criminal cases on board without applying their mind, these cases where the process is considered the punishment produce over time a 'chilling effect', especially on those who wish to investigate or speak about political corruption. The Jayalalithaa regimes of 2001-2006 and 2011-2016 specialized in this strategy of aggressive defence and there can be little doubt that the strategy proved effective.

A rough sketch of Tamil Nadu's grand corruption system goes as follows. Year-round, major payments come into the central warehouse for illicit collections in an astonishing variety of ways. These include calibrated arrangements for levying and sharing bribes, kickbacks, and percentage-based 'rents' received for government collusion with big private operators in bending or breaking laws applicable to the mining of river sand, beach sand and placer minerals, and granite quarrying; pervasive corruption in the power sector ranging from collecting bribes for the arbitrary award of contracts to receiving kickbacks for the purchase of electricity from private parties at exorbitant rates; the collection of kickbacks from the distilleries and breweries supplying 'Indian Made Foreign Liquor' (IMFL) to the Tamil Nadu State Marketing Corporation

Limited (TASMAC); illicit collections from colluding with the import, transport, and handling of coal at inflated cost, often involving benami entities; bribes extracted for giving building approvals, for overlooking violations of building rules, for awarding Public Works Department contracts, and for industrial land allotment from the vast stock of land available with the State Industries Promotion Corporation of Tamilnadu Limited (SIPCOT); corruption in the procurement of pulses for the state's universal public distribution system and in the purchase of eggs for the school midday meal scheme;the extraction of bribes for a vast range of public service appointments, postings, and transfers that are within the government's purview; and pervasive corruption in the education sector.

The list is by no means exhaustive[9]. The ballpark figure that has recently been doing the rounds in political and media circles for first-order payments into the central kitty is ₹200 crore a month, but this is practically impossible to verify.

Another form of corruption and abuse of power came to the fore during (Dravida Munnetra Kazhagam DMK) rule, especially between 2006 and 2011—'land grabbing' through coercion or fraud. When Jayalalithaa returned to power in 2011, her government set up special anti-land grab police cells in all districts and special courts to try land grabbing cases. Hundreds of cases were registered, mostly against DMK functionaries and activists, resulting in complaints of malicious targeting, persecution, and harassment. There can be little doubt that land grabbing took place extensively under DMK rule but it is too much to believe that the AIADMK's leading functionaries, activists, and supporters were not involved in the racketeering. In February 2015, the Madras High Court quashed two government orders (GOs) that had constituted thirty-six anti-land grabbing police cells and set up twenty-three special courts to try land grabbing cases. The GOs were struck down on the ground that they offended Article 14 of the Constitution, which guarantees equality before the law, and Article 21, which safeguards protection of life and personal liberty. The high court judgment pointed out that no principle or guideline had been disclosed by the GOs for selecting and classifying offences and cases, no clear definition of land grabbing had been laid down, and there was the possibility of misuse of the discretionary powers given to the special police cells. This signalled the end of the Jayalalithaa government's crackdown on land grabbing.

Investigating Corruption

The continuing illegal exploitation of Tamil Nadu's abundant natural resources such as beach sand, river sand, bauxite, magnesite, and granite has been a fertile area for journalistic investigation. Some broad-sweep estimates of the scale and costs of corruption involved in this were first presented in a lead article written by Ilangovan Rajasekaran for a cover story in *Frontline* magazine:

> Government sources, who insist on anonymity, estimate the losses…in terms of revenue and degraded assets…at Rs 1.43 lakh crore. Environmentalists put the annual loss to the government from beach sand mining at Rs 20,000 crore to Rs 30,000 crore and from illegal river sand mining at Rs 30,000 crore.[10]

In a meticulous and well-substantiated three-part investigation of river sand mining in Tamil Nadu published in *Scroll*[11], M. Rajshekhar, who followed up the *Frontline* article[12], laid bare a racket that was estimated annually to take out of the state's river beds six crore tonnes of sand valued at ₹24,000 crore, out of which just 1 per cent made its way into the state's coffers. Rajshekhar traced the history of sand mining in the state from the mid-1980s, its evolution from a small-scale activity involving local transporters through a phase when district politicians took over the trade from the transporters to the present stage where a coterie of big private operators in league with top politicians has taken the racket to new levels. The *Scroll* exposé drove home the 'incredibly destructive' social, economic, political, and environmental effects of this system of grand corruption which had however proved to be 'unstoppable'.

In her investigation of beach sand mining operations in Tamil Nadu published in *The Wire*[13], Sandhya Ravishankar exposed a grand corruption racket going on for three decades, involving a nexus between a few mining barons, the government at the highest levels, and state and possibly central officials, and 'costing the exchequer tens of thousands of crores of rupees'. She noted that 'S. Vaikundarajan, owner of V. V. Minerals, the largest sand mining magnate in the country...along with his brothers and close associates have a stranglehold, a virtual monopoly in fact, over beach sand mining in the country'. Under the pressure of journalistic investigation, fact-finding reports by some honest officials, and judicial intervention, the central and state governments 'have begun to choke' the illicit beach sand mining businesses. But Ravishankar's prediction is that the beach sand mining barons, who have 'used their political and financial clout to get their way for three decades' through several changes of regime 'will not go down without a fight'. Whether they will go down at all remains to be seen.

A wealth of data is now available on the mechanics, modus operandi, and devastating effects of illegal granite quarrying in Madurai district, which makes it an ideal candidate for a case study of a powerful and well-oiled system of grand corruption operating at the sub-regional level. How this information came to light, in the face of strenuous political and official obstruction, is itself an interesting story.

In 2011, the Jayalalithaa government, following up campaign rhetoric against the corruption of the preceding DMK regime, sought a report on the 'granite scam' from the administration of Madurai district. But when the district collector, U. Sagayam, an IAS officer known for his independence, submitted a report in May 2012[14] that exposed large-scale illegal quarrying estimated to have caused a loss of ₹16,338 crore to the state and official collusion with the offenders, he was transferred out of his post and the report was suppressed. An exposé by *Puthiya Thalaimurai*, a Tamil news television channel, brought to light the findings of Sagayam's report, and this piece of enterprising journalism helped build up public pressure for fixing responsibility for the losses and taking action against the offenders. The state government was obliged to order a fresh probe into the matter. Sagayam's successor as district collector followed up earnestly before he too was transferred out of the post, in June 2013. Several criminal cases were filed against the lessees for illegal granite quarrying operations and against officials for corruption; seventy-seven quarrying operations were suspended under government orders and thirty-nine quarrying leases were cancelled; and court-ordered proceedings were initiated by the district administration to compute and recover the losses sustained by the government from each delinquent lessee.

However, as Sagayam observed in a report submitted subsequently to the Madras High Court: 'The alacrity with which the Government acted immediately after the media exposure slowly dissipated. Investigations were insincere and the approach was to allow the whole issue to die a natural death. It is probably this failure to go the whole hog to get to the bottom of the issue and examine it in all its dimensions that has led to a sense of scepticism about the intention of the government to take the investigations and prosecutions to its logical end.[15]'

Sagayam's May 2012 report on illegal granite quarrying in Madurai district formed the basis of a public interest litigation seeking a comprehensive investigation of illegal mining and quarrying in thirty-two districts of Tamil Nadu. This, in turn, resulted in a Madras High Court order, in September 2014, appointing Sagayam as Special Officer/Legal Commissioner 'to visit and inspect the mines [in Madurai district] and submit a report to this Court in order to satisfy ourselves that action is being taken at the sites in question'. He was directed to submit his report to the court within two months. The Tamil Nadu government, clearly not pleased with this judicial intervention, adopted delaying tactics. It challenged, unsuccessfully, Sagayam's appointment in the Supreme Court, which was scathing in its observation while dismissing the government's petition against the high court order: 'The facts are eloquent enough to point to the rampant illegal mining in the State. Let him go and inquire.'[16] On 23 November 2015, the IAS officer submitted to the high court a 624-page report, plus a glossary and thousands of pages of annexures, but this is yet to find its way into the public domain.

There is no scope here to go into the details of Special Officer/Legal Commissioner Sagayam's observations, findings, and recommendations, which I have been able to access. But these excerpts from the Executive Summary[17] convey a sense of the 2015 report's potentially explosive impact and why it is unpalatable to the state government:

The field inspections provided a deep insight into the extent of devastation caused due to extensive granite quarrying and the multidimensional illegality involved in the process of mining. It could be seen during inspection that prime agricultural lands were ravaged, water bodies destroyed, pathways obstructed, temples desecrated, sites of archaeological importance vandalised, bio-diversity devastated, environment polluted, gullible villagers displaced, and so on[18].

The widespread nature of such illegalities indicated that such subversion of law occurred only with the tacit and open support and collusion of different levels of the revenue department and bureaucracy, who operated with a sense of impunity, confident that they will never be caught. It is fairly obvious that such deliberate and conscious subversion of law and procedure at the level of the revenue officials occurred because of a well-oiled system of monetary and material patronage; in other words, the existence of a network of corrupt officials, dishonest elected local body leaders like Panchayat Presidents and unscrupulous Mining Lessees ensured that no action was ever taken against the mining interests[19].

The highlight of the entire granite mining episode is the shady dealings resorted to by the Government of Tamil Nadu enterprise viz., TAMIN [Tamil Nadu Minerals Limited]…TAMIN quarries had the best quality of granite and would fetch high prices…[It] introduced a peculiar system of 'Raising Agency in 1984 and Raising-Cum-Sale Agency' in 1998 for quarrying and sale of granites in Government Poramboke quarries. By this system the private players were indirectly allowed to quarry granite in the Government lands under the guise of 'Raising Agency and Raising-Cum-Sale Agency' engaged by…TAMIN.[20]

Sagayam found, further, that the mining barons were not satisfied with the handsome profits that could be made from exporting granite by lawful means in a 'seller's market' to the United States, European, and other developed, countries, and were 'unable to contain their mounting greed' to make superprofits. They resorted to big-time fraud and money laundering, with officialdom at various levels colluding with them[21].

The intrepid IAS officer held the political government fully accountable for the granite quarrying racket:

Such an unprecedented fiscal loss to the Government exchequer besides total destruction of [the] agrarian economy could not have occurred without the active connivance of the Administrative Executives…The Political Executives could have stopped such grave irregularities and sizeable fiscal loss in [the] mining arena. It is sad that nothing concrete was done on their part. There was total systemic failure that was the root cause of all above-mentioned misdeeds[22].

Corruption and 'Populist' or Welfare Schemes

It is a paradox that this system of grand corruption, which had its origins in the early 1980s, has flourished in a relatively developed and reputedly well-administered and progressive state. Part of the explanation for the paradox is that in Tamil Nadu corruption coexists with a substantial basket of well-administered welfare schemes, which themselves involve corruption in a calibrated way. We have already noted the devastating social, economic, political, and environmental effects of corruption in the state's minerals, mining, and quarrying sectors. But there are other types of corruption whose effects can be seen, objectively speaking, to be less damaging or at least mixed.

For example, the administration of Tamil Nadu's school midday meal programme and universal public distribution system can by no means be said to be corruption-free but this has not prevented their being rated as the best in the country for coverage, price, and innovative, foolproof delivery. Likewise, some researchers have found that the practice of panchayat presidents and other village-level officials pocketing small unauthorized amounts deducted from the daily wages paid to members of non-privileged rural households under the Mahatma Gandhi National Rural Employment Guarantee Scheme has not harmed the implementation of the progressive welfare scheme; on the contrary, by providing modest incentives, the practice seems to have helped maximize the reach and effectiveness of a scheme that aims to create a social safety net by providing one hundred days of unskilled wage employment to members of every rural household.

Recent research into 'populism' and 'clientelist' and 'programmatic' politics in Tamil Nadu by Andrew Wyatt[23], Harriss and Wyatt[24], and some others has provided new insights. This research has sought to address the Tamil Nadu political economy 'puzzle'—the question of how populism or welfarism, sustained economic growth, and corruption can coexist to yield relatively successful delivery outcomes. Wyatt[25] takes issue with the way commentators on Indian politics frequently use the term 'populism' to refer to short-term, electorally driven, irresponsible expenditure; he suggests instead that 'the term is more insightfully used when referring to an ideological construct that celebrates the importance of people as an undivided group' and critically examines how the DMK and the AIADMK have adjusted or reworked their populist appeal in the recent period. Looking at the use of material appeals for voter support by the two Dravidian movement parties, Wyatt[26] finds that they have been able to modify their political strategies and strike a new balance between 'clientelist politics, in the form of vote buying, and the distribution of public resources as political patronage', and 'programmatic policies which offer benefits to beneficiaries regardless of political affiliation'. He sees significance in the fact that the provision of such universal benefits has expanded since 2006.

These research findings help us better understand how

pervasive, omnipresent, and systemic corruption, which is the focus of this chapter, fits into the Tamil Nadu political economy puzzle. What is clear is that a balance is constantly sought to be struck, a trade-off sought to be effected, between the costs of political and bureaucratic corruption, the benefits of populism, increasingly through the provision of universal welfare benefits, and pragmatic policies to sustain economic growth. This balancing act, which the AIADMK and the DMK have been adept at performing, goes some way towards explaining why, although corruption can be a potent issue in some elections, anti-corruption movements have not made much headway in Tamil Nadu.

Pre-history of Tamil Nadu's Corruption System

An interesting question is how such a system of political corruption came into being in the first place. Corruption raised its head in Tamil Nadu under Congress auspices in the second half of the 1960s, but it remained sporadic and low key. When the DMK came to power in 1967—a watershed moment in the political history of the state—the reputation of its helmsman, Chief Minister C. N. Annadurai, for personal financial integrity was unimpeachable. For the two years he was in office before his untimely death, he did his best to run a clean government.

The situation changed in the post-Annadurai era when allegations of corruption and a lack of transparency figured prominently in sharpening tensions within the ruling party. In November 1972, following the split in the DMK, M. G. Ramachandran (MGR), leader of the breakaway Anna Dravida Munnetra Kazhagam (ADMK)[27], submitted a memorandum to the President asking for the appointment of a commission of enquiry to look into his allegations of corruption against Chief Minister M. Karunanidhi, several of his cabinet colleagues, and DMK district functionaries and officials who were named for 'abetting the crime of corruption by Ministers'. Soon after this, MGR's ally, M. Kalyanasundaram, a Communist Party of India veteran, submitted two more memoranda carrying corruption charges. Nothing much happened by way of follow-up until the promulgation of the Emergency and the dismissal of the DMK government on 31 January 1976, ostensibly on the issue of corruption. Barely two months before the dismissal, a fourth memorandum had been submitted by two former DMK leaders who had joined MGR's camp.

Within days of the undemocratic dismissal, a Supreme Court judge, Ranjit Singh Sarkaria, was appointed to function as a one-man commission to enquire into the twenty-eight allegations of corruption and misuse of power; most of these charges had been gathering dust for more than three years. The whole exercise, carried out under the authoritarian Emergency regime and featuring selective leaks spiced up by official propaganda, turned out in the end to be a futile affair. In its First Report, submitted on the eve of the March 1977 Lok Sabha election, the Sarkaria Commission of Inquiry held that six of the seven allegations it had looked into had been proved, wholly or in part; and the Indira Gandhi government, which was facing an electoral debacle, let it be known that it would institute legal proceedings against Karunanidhi and his colleagues. Sarkaria had reportedly labelled the dismissed chief minister and his close associates masters of 'scientific corruption'[28], a theme and a phrase Jayalalithaa was to pick up during her successful campaign for the 2011 Tamil Nadu Assembly elections[29].

When the four volumes of the Final Reports of the Commission[30] were eventually published, they turned out to be a damp squib: now most of the twenty-one remaining allegations were held to be groundless or unsubstantiated. The prejudicial political circumstances, the haste with which the 1976 exercise had been conducted, the inconclusive and laboured nature of the evidence turned up, the public perception that all this was a political vendetta enacted through a command quasi-judicial performance, and, above all, the electoral rout of the Emergency regime ensured that the corruption charges against the DMK and its top leader were buried.

The Sarkaria Commission's labours, far from helping to unearth and combat political corruption, served only to undermine the credibility of formal anti-corruption mechanisms, in particular, commissions of enquiry, making them seem like instruments of political vendetta. This paralleled the way forced sterilization during the Emergency set back the family planning programme by at least a decade.

Ironically, the foundations for Tamil Nadu's distinctive corruption system were laid during MGR's second term as chief minister (June 1980-December 1984). The anti-corruption warrior had run a reputedly clean government in his first term (June 1977-February 1980) but it proved too good to last. The day on which TASMAC was incorporated as a company, 23 May 1983, can be regarded as the founding date of Tamil Nadu's scientific system of political corruption. Vesting TASMAC with 'the exclusive privilege of wholesale supply of IMFL for the whole state of Tamil Nadu as per Section 17(C)(1-A)(a) of the Tamilnadu Prohibition Act 1937' proved to be an ingenious idea.

In *The Image Trap*, a study of what made MGR immensely popular among 'the subaltern classes', M. S. S. Pandian argues that, contrary to the image of the charismatic actor-and-politician being openhanded to a fault, the AIADMK government under him regularly 'taxed the poor (and the middle classes) to profit the rich'. Noting that the poor contributed quite heavily to excise revenue, he points out that largely as a consequence of the MGR government relaxing the prohibition on liquor consumption, the share of excise in the total revenue of the state rose sharply, from 1 per cent during 1975-1980 to nearly 14 per cent during 1980-1985. And 80 per cent of this excise revenue came from country liquor, which was mostly consumed by the urban and rural poor. Pandian's comment is telling:

> The manner in which the AIADMK government implemented a perversely unique liquor policy, which profited the liquor manufacturers enormously, is now well-known. It allowed the liquor manufacturers to decide the price at which they would supply Indian Made Foreign Liquor… to…TASMAC… Unlike anywhere else in India, it was not the manufacturers who paid the excise duty on IMFL in Tamil Nadu but the state government, via…TASMAC. Again, the AIADMK government exempted the liquor manufacturers from paying any excise duty on rectified spirit.[31]

The creation of TASMAC and vesting it with a monopoly of wholesale supply of Indian Made Foreign Liquor (IMFL) was widely perceived to be an innovative way of financing the state's welfare schemes, especially MGR's ambitious nutritious midday meal programme of July 1982, which quickly expanded to become India's largest in terms of beneficiaries and a model for other states. Less known at the time was the stream of illicit revenues that began to flow from the favoured owners of distilleries and breweries manufacturing the liquor into a political fund that was now at the disposal of the chief minister. It was the inauguration of grand corruption in Tamil Nadu—a corrupt set of acts committed at the top level of government that manipulated and distorted policies (prohibition and its relaxation), institutions (TASMAC as the sole wholesale supplier of IMFL), and processes (price-rigging, sweetheart deals, nepotism) to enable leaders to benefit at the expense of the public good.

Two decades after the creation of TASMAC, an AIADMK government headed by Jayalalithaa vested it with the exclusive privilege of retail vending of Indian Made Foreign Spirits (IMFS), thus expanding the scope for corruption through total control over the distribution and sale of liquor in the state, supposedly in pursuit of prohibition policy goals. There is a substantial journalistic and legal literature on the controversies surrounding TASMAC. The allegations include the violation or circumventing of labour laws[32]; crony capitalism in the whole sector[33]; appointments and transfers made in state-run liquor shops on the basis of fake recommendation letters[34]; and damaging economic, social, and health effects among 'the low-earning echelons of Tamil society', including an estimated 10 million addicts[35]. Today the two dominant parties are publicly committed to introducing prohibition in the state, the AIADMK in stages and the DMK totally. On the other hand, TASMAC has been a high-yielding cash cow for the state government. Its total revenues, comprising excise revenue and sales tax, from the sale of liquor soared from ₹3639.93 crore in 2003-2004 to ₹14,965.42 crore in 2010-2011 to ₹25,845.58 crore in 2015-2016[36]. Aside from the well-known complications and hazards of implementing a policy of prohibition, it is not clear how the huge revenues, legal and illicit, that will be lost can be made up.

In the three decades following MGR's death, the

two dominant parties in the state took turns to develop, refine, upgrade, and scale up the corruption system put in place in the early 1980s. Escalating political and electoral financing needs, the desire of political leaders and their kin for personal enrichment to levels previously unheard of in the state, and the abundance of opportunity that charisma, stardom, and mass popularity offered strong leaders in a relatively developed state with decent economic growth rates combined to make Tamil Nadu's system of grand corruption what it is today, something akin to an autonomous subformation within a social formation.

Jayalalithaa's last five years in office saw rule-bound scientific corruption escalate. As we have seen, she had been twice convicted and then acquitted on appeal on corruption charges, and at the time of her death she was awaiting the Supreme Court of India's final verdict in the disproportionate assets case. But this stressful experience does not seem to have acted as a deterrent to taking grand corruption to new heights. During the state's Legislative Assembly election campaign in April 2016, Amit Shah, the BJP president, accused Jayalalithaa's government of being 'the most corrupt' in the country[37]. Five months later, soon after the Chief Minister had been hospitalized, a senior BJP minister confided in me that when it came to corruption Tamil Nadu ranked 'Number One' in India and that this assessment was based not on hearsay or general impressions, but on concrete evidence available with the central government.

An article published in *The Caravan* soon after

Jayalalithaa's death offered an interesting explanation for how she had got away with her mode of governance:

> Nothing stuck to her, neither corruption charges nor charges of being an autocrat, or for that matter, accusations of land-grabbing. This is because in her person, she reconciled popular need and state action, and to doubt her meant that one was casting aspersions on the notion of popular sovereignty itself. This explains all those defamation cases, and her unwillingness to listen to criticism, unless it appealed to her…she existed as the very source of popular legitimacy, never mind her disinterest in democracy.[38]

This insight has wider and troubling significance for the fight against corruption in India. When a strong and charismatic leader with mass appeal and a loyal organization to support her or him makes a bold stand invoking the notion of popular sovereignty, anti-corruption campaigns rarely succeed in making a major political impact. In such cases campaigners against corruption face two difficult challenges: they need to prove corruption through robust evidence; and they need to persuade millions of voters that popular legitimacy is no defence, and the notion of popular sovereignty no argument, against proven corruption in a social environment where people believe that most politicians are corrupt.

To return to the Tamil Nadu story. It is now clear that while Jayalalithaa was hospitalized and fighting for her life, the BJP government was biding its time to strike. The opening shot was fired three days after the Chief Minister's death. Closely coordinated income tax raids unearthed a black money racket operated by J. Sekhar Reddy and K. Sreenivasulu[39], two politically connected businessmen engaged in river sand mining and construction in Tamil Nadu and allegedly enjoying a cosy relationship with senior bureaucrats and the top AIADMK leadership. With the Enforcement Directorate and the Central Bureau of Investigation moving into action, cases filed under the Prevention of Money Laundering Act and the Prevention of Corruption against the businessmen, their associates, and unnamed public servants, and several arrests made, it became clear that this was no ordinary income tax raid.

With the trail leading straight to Chief Secretary P. Rama Mohana Rao, income tax searches were conducted at his residence, other relevant premises, and, most dramatically, his office in the State Secretariat[40]. Moving in without informing the Chief Minister and engaging Central Reserve Police Force (CRPF) personnel in the income tax raids[41] seemed to be designed to send a tough message to the state government—'we can do this to any of you and we know most of you are sitting ducks'. Few, however, could disagree with the view, articulated among others by the displaced Chief Secretary of Tamil Nadu, that had Chief Minister Jayalalithaa been alive and in charge at Fort St George, the central government would not have dared to resort to such action.

The political situation in Tamil Nadu took a series of dramatic turns in the weeks following the death of

Jayalalithaa. The ruling party, despite being able to muster a majority through dubious means on the floor of the Legislative Assembly, was riven with internal dissension, severely weakened, and in danger of losing its popular legitimacy. In early April 2017, there was more political drama following raids conducted by the income tax department in twenty-one places in Chennai and eleven elsewhere in the state belonging to Dr C. Vijaya Baskar, minister for health, and his associates[42]. The raids were based on information received on tax evasion and distribution of cash during the by-election in Chennai's Dr Radhakrishnan Nagar Assembly constituency, which had fallen vacant with Jayalalithaa's death. With the income tax department forwarding the incriminating information, which suggested that apart from the Health Minister, the central figure, several political leaders belonging to the ruling party were involved in a racket to distribute cash totalling ₹89 crore as bribes to voters in the constituency, to the Election Commission of India, the latter moved swiftly to cancel the by-election.[43]

The fourteen-page order of the ECI[44] setting out the circumstances and reasons behind the cancellation of the by-election tells a sorry story of how, despite adopting extraordinary measures, the constitutional authority could not prevail against 'a huge and systematic design to distribute money to voters in order to induce/bribe them to influence their voting behaviour.' Nothing in the order suggests that the corrupted by-election would have been cancelled if the income tax department had not acted on the information that came fortuitously to hand. The ECI finally consoled itself with the thought that top political leaders could not feign ignorance of such illegal activities by their party candidates, especially in some states that have 'excelled in innovating more and more subtle ways to circumvent the statutory provisions enacted by Parliament to curb the menace of money power in elections' and that 'the innovative ways which the political parties and their leaders at the top echelons have devised to bypass the law' needed to be 'dealt with a heavy hand'.

What is the future of the state's grand corruption system? Will it remain intact, continue to flourish, or will it prove to be soft and vulnerable and disintegrate in the face of attacks by the opposition, investigations by journalists and official agencies, judicial intervention, and, above all, the erosion of popular legitimacy?

Nobody can answer these questions with any confidence, but the opportunity beckons. Now is the time to target Tamil Nadu's scientific system of political corruption, not by underhand political manipulation from the centre, not by making exaggerated claims and allegations, but with precision and detail and by marshalling anti-corruption resources and campaigning actively on the issue among the people. It may be too much to expect a grand corruption system that has been decades in the making to be dismantled any time soon but from a democratic standpoint, it would be irresponsible not to make a resourceful and well-prepared strategic charge.

CONCLUSION

WHAT CAN BE DONE ABOUT CORRUPTION AND SCAMS?

This book began by noting that there is no such thing as political corruption as a self-contained category. If the objective is to understand corruption in India in its pervasiveness, its omnipresence, and its multifariousness, so that something meaningful and effective can be done about it, it needs to be approached as a problem not just of politics or the economy or society, not to mention the moral sphere—but of political economy in its profound sense. Consistent with this understanding, there have been two larger themes running through this book. I have attempted to harmonize them, or at least prevent them from going out of control while contending with each other.

The first theme is the intractability of corruption under the prevailing circumstances, which is to say that without making deep-going and radical changes to India's political economy it will not be possible to prevent and eliminate corruption. I hope the arguments made in this book have been able to demonstrate the validity and the truth of this principal proposition.

The second and, in a sense, the counter theme running through the book is that it would be unreasonable to suggest that the fight against corruption in India must wait for a revolution, or at least until a radical restructuring of the prevailing socio-economic system occurs. Combating corruption is decidedly a challenge of the here and now and it must be taken up as one of India's important national tasks, along with other priority tasks. I hope this too has been brought home in this book.

It is important to remember that corruption is not one mode of moral and social behaviour. There is corruption and corruption, and we need to disaggregate and differentiate it if we are going to get some purchase on it. I have suggested that this is best done by looking at the effects of specific types of corruption in society. When we do this, with the help of data gathered from the field, we can distinguish corruption that is grossly damaging from other types that are not as damaging or far less damaging. Further, since the challenge is on many fronts, it must be responded to strategically, in stages, and with an eye to weakening and undermining corruption's base rather than concentrating on its symptoms. All this suggests that working out a hierarchy and sequence of anti-corruption initiatives and actions is the key.

But first let us get some intellectual cobwebs out of the way when we ask ourselves why corruption needs to be combated and eliminated. Why does India, an extremely unjust and exploitative society in socio-economic terms, which has a greater mass of poverty and basic deprivation of every kind than any other country in the world, need to rid itself of corruption? The answer is not as obvious as it appears. It cannot be that India needs to do this to protect and promote economic growth, because there is no robust evidence to show that as a general proposition corruption is incompatible with, or harms, growth. Nor is there evidence that can hold up at the national level to show that corruption exacerbates inequality and deprivation in society, or is an obstacle to poverty alleviation and development.

Nor can unaffordable welfare costs be cited as the reason India needs to rid itself of corruption. Remember the finding in the well-known illustrative case taken up and adjudicated by traditional rent-seeking theory? It is that corruption, being close to a pure transfer, is a less wasteful form of rent-seeking than competitive lobbying. As we saw in Chapter 4, this finding has been challenged by some rent-seeking theorists whose estimates of the welfare costs are quite different. But the point has been made: worse things happen in the political economy than corruption.

Does all this sound like an apologia for corruption? It should not, if you have followed the argument made in this book closely and with an open mind. Let me state this clearly and unequivocally: Corruption is bad and totally unacceptable from any democratic and progressive standpoint. But it is a normal, not an abnormal, condition within the political economy of capitalism. Cronyism exacerbates the condition but corruption, understood as an integral part of the omnipresence of private interests in the public sphere, including political life, is endemic to all forms of capitalism.

Cassius's wise and profound words

> The fault, dear Brutus, is not in our stars,
> But in ourselves, that we are underlings.[1]

have salience and application here. The fault—the determinants of mass poverty and deprivation, growing inequality, economic underperformance, and social injustice and oppression—is not in a pathological condition, a deviation from an ideologically imagined norm, called corruption. The determinate fault lies in India's capitalist system, which has developed a high degree of monopoly, is enmeshed with international finance capital, is caste-ridden, and coexists with vestiges of semi-feudalism and its mutations. The fault lies also in 'ourselves', masters as well as underlings in this system. The remedies therefore must be sought deep in the structure of India's political economy.

Keeping the general limitation as well as the guidelines mentioned above in mind, I categorize what can be done to combat corruption under nine broad heads. These proposals cover laws, enforcement capacity, policies, institutions, regulation, vigilance, the private sector, journalism, and politics.

1. *Action needed on the legislative front*: The Prevention of Corruption Act 1988 is India's principal anti-corruption law but unlike the UK Bribery Act 2010, it is not comprehensive in its coverage of corruption offences. The PCA comes into play only if a public servant is alleged to have committed a corruption offence. This means corruption, however flagrant or damaging, committed by private individuals and companies cannot be prosecuted under India's main anti-corruption law unless the essential ingredient of a public servant committing the offence of corruption, as narrowly defined in the Act, is present in the case. The criminal cases against the private individuals and shell companies shown to have received percentage-based payoffs disguised as 'commissions' from Bofors AB in connection with the Indian howitzer deal collapsed because the CBI failed to provide evidence of any money trail leading to the public servants involved in the case.

   The PCA (Amendment) Bill 2013 was introduced with the explanation that it was necessitated by India's ratification of the United Nations Convention Against Corruption, international practice on the treatment of the offences of bribery and corruption, judicial pronouncements, and the need to bring the country's anti-corruption jurisprudence in line with current international practice and the standards set by the UN Convention. The implication was that the amendments would make the PCA a tougher law with expanded scope. But as we saw in Chapter 3, what the amendment bill, which is pending in Parliament, seeks to do is to weaken the PCA. This process of diluting the PCA, clearly at the behest of concerned politicians and bureaucrats, needs to be reversed. Further, three key provisions of the UN Convention—bribery of foreign public officials, bribery in the private sector, and compensation for those who have suffered damage as a result of an act of corruption—need to be inducted as soon as possible into India's anti-corruption legal armoury, if not into a radically recast PCA, then as separate legislation.

The Lokpal and Lokayuktas Act 2013, which has been gathering dust from January 2014, when it was notified, must be operationalized and a truly independent Lokpal put in place. The official reason given for the delay in November 2016 to a sceptical Supreme Court was that the Selection Committee for the appointment of the chairperson and members of the Lokpal could not be constituted because there was no official leader of the Opposition in the Lok Sabha and the amending bill meant to address the issue was pending in parliament. This excuse has worn thin. The Lokpal, despite its inherent functional limitations, is the best chance India has had in seven decades to put in place an independent central mechanism to investigate and prosecute corruption offences. Getting this institutional mechanism to work brooks no further delay.

The Whistleblowers Protection Act, which has been lying dormant in the statute book since May 2014, must be notified without further delay. The 2015 Amendment Bill, which prohibits disclosure to the competent authority of information relating to a public servant's alleged corruption or misuse of power or discretion, or attempt to commit a criminal offence, if such disclosure contains information falling under ten broad categories, is a regressive step. If whistleblowing is to be meaningful, the number of prohibited categories must be pared down from the proposed ten to a bare minimum.

To sum up, India's legal framework for dealing with pervasive, omnipotent, and variegated corruption is far from adequate; and there is a lot of legislative and political work to be done if the country's anti-corruption laws can be said to be in line with its obligations under the UN Convention Against Corruption. Living up to India's obligations under the UN Convention within a specified time frame can be made a vital plank in the fight against corruption.

2. *Action needed to overcome the lack of enforcement capacity*: Corruption theorists and empirical researchers generally agree that for India, developing enforcement capacity is even more important than strengthening

the existing laws against corruption. Sukhtankar and Vaishnav are on solid ground when they identify the lack of enforcement capacity as a key driver of pervasive corruption in India. As we saw in Chapter 3, they report from their research into corruption that the lack of enforcement capacity can be related to such factors as the 'overburdened, inadequately staffed, and often poorly equipped' government agencies in charge of administration and law and order; the small number of government employees relative to the population and the enormous burdens placed on them to enforce the large number of schemes and regulations in place; political interference and meddling; unfilled job vacancies, especially in the police services and in courts (from the subordinate to the high court level); and the backlog of cases that has clogged up the judicial system.[2]

Empirical research such as the Commonwealth Human Rights Initiative's study[3] of what happens to corruption cases across the land, which we cited in Chapter 3, shows that enforcement of anti-corruption laws figures among the lowest priorities of India's political-legal system. This has to do with several factors, notably the entrenched political culture of immunity at the bar of public prosecution, the dependence of police investigators and official prosecutors on their political masters, and dogged political and bureaucratic resistance to the enforcement of the anti-corruption laws at various levels. Add to this the problem of the law's delays, which features the hijacking of the adjudicative process by defence lawyers, the failure of the judiciary to observe strict timelines, and an enormous case backlog, and we can see that the problem is unmanageable.

It follows from this analysis that the solution to the problem of weak enforcement capacity is not less government, but more and better government. This necessarily means dramatically increased and qualitatively enhanced staffing of the various arms of the state, especially the administrative services, the police, and the judiciary. Developing better, more transparent, and more accountable delivery mechanisms to distribute basic entitlements, especially welfare goods and services, directly to the people is also a vital part of building enforcement capacity and preventing corruption.

When we address the challenge of developing enforcement capacity in a society where mass deprivation and food insecurity are central and inescapable realities, it is only natural that larger social questions and, in particular, issues of entitlement and justice intrude into and dominate the corruption debate. For example, a policy question that has huge implications for food security, especially in rural India, is how best to distribute adequate and nutritious food to those who are most in need of it. The answer is that for a public distribution system (PDS), the cleanest and most efficient way is not targeting, but universal provision. This finding is theoretically sound and has been validated by long-term Indian experience.

India's PDS, which is the joint responsibility of the central and state governments, is a gigantic enterprise. After the adoption and notification of the National Food Security Act 2013, the stated aim has been to cover up to two-thirds of the national population, that is, about 800 million people. The PDS works through 528,000 fair price shops spread across thirty-three states and union territories[4]; and it claimed an estimated ₹145, 339 crore allocation for food subsidy (0.9 per cent of GDP) in the 2017-2018 central budget[5].

There is plenty of empirical evidence to show that wrongful exclusion from targeted PDS provision extracts a much higher human and social cost than undeserved inclusion, considering that those unjustly excluded are often from the poorest, the least literate, and the most vulnerable sections of society. Considerations of justice aside, economists have shown that leakages and corruption tend to be greater in a targeted public distribution system than in a universal one[6]. Using data from different rounds of the National Sample Survey, Himanshu and Abhijit Sen[7], as well as Jean Dreze and Reetika Khera[8], find that leakages from the PDS are lower in states with universal or near-universal provision, such as Tamil Nadu and Chhattisgarh, than in states with narrow targeting. They also show that over time leakages have declined in states where coverage has improved. Analyzing the costs of targeting, Madhura Swaminathan explains:

> Targeting can…create an incentive to cheat. In particular, when targeting is by means of administrative methods such as means testing, then the scope of misuse rises. In this respect, narrow targeting is likely to be worse than broad targeting for the following reasons. When the number of eligible persons is reduced, there are…a larger number of non-eligible persons who may try to cheat. Similarly, when resources are restricted, more cheating may occur to gain access to the limited resources available.[9]

Unfortunately, notwithstanding the promise held by the National Food Security Act 2013, political India for the most part has gone in the reverse direction to what has been shown to be the just and most beneficial policy course. Targeting has become the rule and universal provision the exception, with Tamil Nadu and Chhattisgarh being the only states that still believe in universal or near-universal provision. NITI Aayog, the central government's premier 'think tank' which has replaced the Planning Commission, has actually proposed a reduction in food subsidies as a proportion of GDP through better targeting and rationalisation measures[10]. This retrogressive policy needs to be reversed to prevent and eliminate costly errors of exclusion as well as leakages and corruption in public distribution systems across the land.

It can be seen from this that a strategy for building enforcement capacity to tackle pervasive corruption cannot stand aside from larger questions of entitlement and justice in society, but must necessarily engage with them. Overcoming the lack of enforcement capacity in a country as large, as diverse, and as complex as India will call for the deployment of massive financial and human resources as well as deep institutional reform in several areas. But unless this task is taken up as a top policy priority, the battle against corruption will be lost at the starting gate.

3. *The need for stricter, cleaner, and more effective regulation*: Corruption researchers influenced by rent-seeking theory tend to pin the blame for pervasive corruption on regulatory controls and complexity. But this is to misdiagnose the problem and fall into an ideological trap. A deeper examination of the relationship between regulation and corruption would show that it is not regulation or regulatory complexity that is the villain, but regulatory misconduct when it is incentivized and constantly reproduced by the system. Under liberalization, the state plays a different kind of role than it did earlier in a dirigiste system. It actively supports the entry and domination of corporate capital, Indian and foreign, in the economy; and as part of such a strategy it goes all out to provide big business privileged access to scarce resources, often

to the detriment of the petty production sector. It is not as though regulation is done away with under liberalization. Regulators are constituted for various sectors but with fewer checks and balances in place. Under such a regime, it is relatively easy for big capital to suborn the regulatory authorities and the politicians who oversee them to do its bidding.

What is clear is that the solution to the problem of pervasive corruption cannot be 'de-regulation' or the state vacating the 'commanding heights' of the economy or abandoning the field to market forces. The answer is better regulation that ensures that decision-making is subject to due process and is accountable and monitorable. It is possible that a sector-by-sector analysis will show up some fields where lighter or less heavy-handed regulation may be desirable, among other things, to reduce corruption. But there are several fields, such as telecommunications, oil and gas, land and real estate, mining, the power sector, and defence, where stricter, cleaner, and more transparent regulation and the no-nonsense enforcement of rules, with heavy penalties for intentional violations, are likely to produce positive results for the fight against corruption.

4. *Raising the visibility of corporate and private sector fraud*: This rarely figures in mainstream media and public discourse on corruption but it must be recognized as one of corruption's most widely prevalent and toxic forms. There is a mass of evidence, including

recent evidence thrown up by surveys conducted by professional agencies, that shows that corporate fraud, bribery, and other forms of corruption and malfeasance have been on the increase during the past few years and that India ranks among the countries where corporate fraud is most pervasive. No worthwhile lessons have been learnt by the political system from its experience of dealing with an unending series of corporate and private sector scandals beginning with the Harshad Mehta security scam of 1992 and escalating to dizzying levels of wrongdoing of various kinds. On the contrary, these scandals have exposed an extensive network of delinquent regulators, politicians, bureaucrats, banks, and other institutions that have enabled and, in several cases, connived with the scamsters in shaping these mega-scandals. Even more than the spectacular scams, it is the endemic, pervasive, and deepening nature of corruption in India's corporate sector that demands special attention. Democratic movements must work to raise the visibility of corporate fraud and corruption as a public issue, expose its relationship and links to politics, and demonstrate its centrality to the fight against corruption.

5. *Reforming and cleansing political finance and electoral funding:* Political finance is often described by anti-corruption campaigners and journalists as the 'fountain-head' of corruption in India. But this characterization is not just superficial; it turns reality

on its head and overlooks the deeply complicit and interlocked nature of the relationship between big business and politics. As we saw in Chapter 6, the counter view is put forward by the CPI (M) leader and ideologue Prakash Karat: 'the fountain-head of corruption is big business and the neo-liberal policies'; 'it is the illegal money generated by big business and the corporates which has corrupted the political system and not the other way around'; and under a corrupt neo-liberal regime, 'politics becomes business and business is conducted through politics'[11]. There can be little doubt about which characterization accurately describes the Indian situation.

However, the differences in understanding the sources of corruption need not obscure the essential truth that the Indian political system is corrupt to the core, with highly damaging effects. Political finance is a larger issue than electoral funding and, understandably, the latter attracts more practical attention because it is a more immediate issue.

As I noted in Chapter 2, the Election Commission of India has been praised for planning and holding democratic elections in the face of formidable odds but it has completely failed to prevent the corruption of the electoral process through wholesale violations of legal spending limits by political parties holding vast stocks of unaccounted money. Vote-buying with unaccounted cash, which is now standard practice in state assembly and Lok Sabha elections, has highly damaging effects. It eats into the vitals of parliamentary democracy, spreads corruption and cynicism in society, and undermines civic values.

The hundreds of crores of rupees the big parties are able to spend on advertisements, chartering private aircraft and helicopters, and other big-ticket items during elections do not attract the expenditure limits set for candidates. By denying the smaller parties a level playing field, this major flaw in the election law detracts seriously from the democratic character of Indian elections. The Election Commission has been criticized from the Left for its class bias: failing to check the power of big money in the electoral process, it concentrates on targeting 'small donations in cash from…ordinary people'; and it prohibits the use of posters and banners for election propaganda 'which hamper…electioneering by parties with limited financial resources, but encourages parties to advertise on television and print media and put up expensive hoardings'[12].

Meanwhile, the literature on electoral reform, already large, keeps growing. It features proposals put forward by the Election Commission over the years; recommendations by commissions, including the Law Commission of India, and committees; judgments of the Supreme Court of India and high courts; scholarly papers; data-backed analyses, reports, and advocacy material published by the Association for Democratic Reforms and other non-governmental organizations; and hundreds of articles in the press. The reform proposals range from a ban on corporate contributions to parties and candidates contesting elections to state funding of elections through a National Election Trust controlled by the ECI to moving to a system of proportional representation to keep election expenditure in check. But lacking political support, these progressive ideas have failed to take off.

Banning corporate funding of political parties has long been seen as the radical solution to the problem of corrupt political finance. Companies, especially big ones, fund political parties in anticipation of, or in return for, privileges or favours; in other words, corporate funding of parties takes place because it is 'rent-seeking'. As a general proposition, this is incontestable but it will be extraordinarily difficult to get the dominant political parties, national as well as regional, to back the radical solution.

In fact, the current trends in the polity seem to favour incentivizing and encouraging corporate funding of politics on an increasing scale and in an opaque way. The changes in the rules of the game announced by Finance Minister Arun Jaitley in his budget speech of 1 February 2017[13], which have been taken much further by the Finance Act 2017[14], bear this out.

While the government has accepted the Election Commission's suggestion to lower the limit on anonymous cash donations from ₹20,000 to ₹2,000, the other changes made by the Finance Act 2017, in one sweep to the Companies Act 2013[15], the Income Tax Act 1961[16], the Representation of the People Act 1951[17], and the Reserve Bank of India Act 1934,[18] will make it much easier for companies to make unlimited contributions to political parties in a non-transparent, anonymous way.

First, the provision in the Companies Act that the total amount a company could contribute to political parties in any financial year should not exceed 7.5 per cent of its average net profits during the three immediately preceding years has been deleted. Now there is no limit to the political contributions a company can make in a financial year irrespective of its financial performance. The only condition is that all donations above the anonymous cash contribution limit of ₹2,000 must be made by cheque or through digital payments or by using electoral bonds, which are in the nature of bearer bonds.

Second, the provision in the Act that a company should disclose in its profit and loss account all contributions made by it to political parties during the financial year, with particulars of the total amount contributed and the names of the beneficiary parties, has been substituted by a provision that a company needs to disclose only the total amount contributed by it to political parties in the financial year. There will be no need to name the beneficiary political parties.

Third, the Finance Act 2017 has amended the RBI Act to enable the central government to authorize any scheduled bank to issue electoral bonds under a scheme notified by the government. 'Under this scheme,' the Finance Minister had explained in his budget speech, 'a donor could purchase bonds from authorised banks against cheque and digital payments only. They shall be redeemable only in the designated account of a registered political party. These bonds will be redeemable within the prescribed time limit from issue of bond.' His rationale for introducing electoral bonds was that donors to political parties had expressed reluctance to 'contribute by cheque or other transparent means as it would disclose their identity and entail adverse consequences'[19]. Subsequently, the Finance Minister clarified that the idea was for the RBI to authorize a particular bank to issue the bonds, which would be redeemable 'within a short period—let us say, four weeks of its purchase', because otherwise they would turn into 'a parallel currency'[20]. Jaitley justified the overall changes made in the Finance Act as being aimed at giving 'some protection to identities [of donors], expanding the constituency of donors, and encouraging clean money' coming to politics[21]. These changes in the regulation of political finance have drawn a lot of criticism: for making electoral funding more opaque, for making it easier for parties to get larger corporate funding, for opening 'the floodgates' for corporate money to flow into 'the ruling party's coffers,' and for providing a new way of legitimizing bribery, because a company winning a government contract, which would have earlier paid a bribe using black money, can now legally pay a kickback of, say, ten per cent as a donation to the ruling party through the electoral bonds route, 'with no questions asked'[22].

It is not the legality or illegality of the corporate funding of political parties but the quid pro quo, potential or actual, built into the funding that is of primary concern here. If the financial contribution can be kept opaque, the existence of a quid pro quo element can remain a secret between the giver and the receiver. To make matters worse, there is no reason to think that crony and other cash-rich businesses seeking big favours from ruling parties will stop using the traditional under-the-table, unaccounted cash route to make their contributions.

Given these regressive trends, the prospects for reforming and cleansing electoral and political finance in the conceivable future are dim. The only way to start countering these trends is agenda-building through political mobilization and sensitizing the news media and public opinion to what is at stake. This will take time and a huge amount of work on the ground.

6. *The need for judicial accountability in adjudicating corruption cases*: I do not propose to go into the vexed question of how to prevent and eliminate corruption in the

judiciary, and especially the higher judiciary. Although that subject is of great political interest and is also relevant to the issues addressed in this book, dealing with it calls for specialized study and knowledge that is beyond my competence. I will confine myself to the question of judicial accountability in adjudicating corruption cases efficiently and within reasonable time frames. In Chapter 3, I cited a telling comment by N. S. Nigam, a law scholar, that 'the *Jayalalithaa* judgment is a stark reminder that the most intractable problem in tackling corruption in India lies in the hijacking of the adjudicative process by the lawyers of the accused, and the failure on the part of the judiciary to observe strict timelines'. It follows that the trial courts, the high courts, and the Supreme Court of India must be made accountable for their contribution to the law's avoidable delays and, in particular, for failure to observe strict timelines in adjudicating cases. In this connection, the possibility of imposing statutory time limits on judicial decisions in corruption cases at all levels needs to be examined.

7. *The need to develop capabilities to anticipate and prevent corruption in, and exercise systematic vigilance over, high-risk, vulnerable sectors*: The prevention of corruption, especially grand corruption and cronyism, requires hard work on several fronts, but the technologies and tools are available[23]. They include data mining, which can be used to audit procurement processes and 'identify red flags, patterns of collusion, and false

information' and to spot 'corrupt intent' in payments and transactions through data visualization; anti-corruption software designed to 'detect and respond to fraud'; big data, which opens the way for predictive analysis and visualization of suspicious trends, patterns, and relationships; forensic auditing tools, which can be effective in mitigating corruption risk; and mobile applications, which make it possible 'to harness data and gain faster insights'[24]. It goes without saying that these tools can make a worthwhile difference only if there is the political and societal will and mass-based action on the ground to prevent and combat corruption.

Empowered vigilance systems for high-risk, vulnerable, and crony sectors like mining and land allocation recommend themselves as a way of preventing, and minimizing the damage from, corruption in these sectors. By blowing the whistle on unclean and suspicious transactions as soon as they are detected, vigilance can help speed up the process of investigating and prosecuting corruption offences, especially if an independent Lokpal and independent Lokayuktas, as envisaged in the 2013 Act, can get to work. But here again, politics and the performance of two institutions, the police and the judiciary, will be the key determinants of success or failure.

For exercising vigilance against grand corruption, a sectoral approach is likely to work best: begin by identifying the industrial and service sectors that are highly exposed or vulnerable to corruption; these are often crony sectors. *The Economist*, which compiled a crony capitalism index for twenty-two countries, identified ten major 'rent-seeking sectors': casinos; coal, palm oil, and timber; defence; deposit-taking banking and investment banking; infrastructure and pipelines; oil, gas, chemicals, and other energy; ports and airports; real estate and construction; steel, other metals, mining, and commodities; and utilities and telecommunications services[25]. This can serve as a guide for India.

Interestingly, the list of twenty-eight major twenty-first century corruption scandals in India compiled by Sukhtankar and Vaishnav, which we discussed in Chapter 1, implicates mining, land allocation, real estate, construction, telecom and information technology, defence, financial services, and food grain distribution and export as sectors exposed to grand corruption aggregating hundreds of billions of dollars[26]. If we go by the information available from some states starting with Tamil Nadu, the power and utilities sector can be added to this shortlist. Colour-coded lists of business and government sectors and sub-sectors that are exposed to grand corruption—including a red list denoting maximum vulnerability—can be compiled on the strength of available data and intelligence, especially revenue intelligence, and credible news media reports. If the government or official agencies won't compile such lists, a collaborative approach involving independent research centres, non-government organizations, and the news media should be up to the task.

After the information is verified, the lists should be made public and given wide publicity. Since the colour-coded lists will, in the first instance, identify vulnerable sectors exposed to grand corruption, rather than companies or individuals, the risk of defamation proceedings being launched against the authors of the lists will be minimized. Even if the offending companies or individuals are named after careful verification of the information received, a public interest defence will be available in the event of defamation proceedings being launched.

8. *What journalism can do for the fight against corruption*: Some of the finest work done by the Indian press, historically and in contemporary times, is its investigation and exposé of political corruption, ministerial misconduct, and government misdeeds, including those that cause immense damage to the lives of working people. Corruption in its myriad forms and tremendous scale presents limitless investigative opportunities to India's news media, which now comprise newspapers, news television, radio, and the new digital media and have enormous reach and presumed influence in society. The news media can use the burgeoning social media channels with discretion to do 'open journalism' that crowd-sources information on corruption and then verifies it through the application of professional

standards. Exposés of corruption tend to empower the news media by enabling them to win strong public support for the work they do.

In the three decades since the Bofors investigation began, there has been an ebb and flow of investigative journalism and related to this, but separate from it, an ebb and flow of public engagement with the results of investigative journalism. There have been many investigations on issues of significance, done in the public interest, although the general impression is that these investigations have not had anything like the impact Bofors had on national politics.

The 2010 exposé by *Open* magazine and *Outlook* of an unsavoury nexus between politicians, corporates, and journalists, based on the leaked Nira Radia 'tapes', actually 140 digital audio recordings of telephone conversations secretly done by the income tax department in 2008-2009, showed for the first time in India what digital platforms could do for the presentation of a mass of evidence turned up by journalistic enterprise. What the online platform made possible in a way that could not be matched by printed newspapers or even television was that instead of relying solely on the journalist's interpretation and opinion, serious readers and listeners could now make up their own minds. During the Bofors investigation in the analogue age, *The Hindu* was able to print in facsimile form about 200 items of documentary evidence, spread over whole pages. Today a newspaper would be able to publish online a hundred times that number without taxing the reader or taking up too much space.

Indian news television has also contributed actively to the investigation of corruption and abuse of power, but the obsessive reliance by many television reporters on 'stings' using hidden cameras and microphones has narrowed its vision and constrained its approach to the core task of investigation. The problem of the growing use of deception in journalistic investigation leads straight to another issue—'trial by the media', which has been a complaint heard frequently over the past decade. This poses a dilemma for the news media because the line between aggressive investigation of corruption and implicitly judging the people and organizations under investigation to be corrupt before clinching evidence is in hand is thin. It can be argued that all long-drawn-out journalistic investigations, where exposés of alleged corruption and wrongdoing are unveiled in instalments, amount to trial by the media. While such extreme views can be discounted, India's news media organizations need to put in place safeguards, including codes of investigative practice, to prevent unjust trial by the media.

In the digital age, while the quality and range of investigations are not necessarily better than what they were half a century ago, the reach of major work on issues of importance has become global in a way that could not have been imagined in the analogue world. Consider the unprecedented transnational significance of the Panama Papers, the year-long collaborative investigation involving more than a hundred news organizations around the world into 'the sprawling secretive industry of offshore that the world's rich and powerful use to hide assets and skirt rules by setting up front companies in far-flung jurisdictions'[27]. The International Consortium of Investigative Journalists, which decided in early 2017 to spin off from its parent organization, the Center for Public Integrity, and become a fully independent organization with the goal of 'producing the world's best cross-border journalism', has recently announced that it was working with more than 500 journalists to continue the investigation into the offshore finance industry, and launched an appeal for crowdfunding[28]. The *Indian Express*, a partner in the investigative consortium, has taken the lead in exposing the Indian involvement in offshore; a large number of Indian nationals have been named in the Panama Papers and, according to press reports, 415 Indians are under scrutiny by the multi-agency Special Task Force that was set up by the central government soon after the Panama Papers were released in April 2016[29].

But covering corruption and abuse of power should be much more than being able to work securely with confidential sources and large datasets, or use the new technologies and tools available to the trained digital journalist. Above all, investigations need to be visualized within a broader historical and conceptual framework. The long-term Indian press experience suggests two extremely valuable functions that the country's best newspapers have performed in modern and contemporary times. These functions may be termed (a) the *credible-informational* and (b) the *critical-investigative-adversarial*. Performed over time, the two central functions working together build trust in the press and a public culture of valuing these roles develops. There are also valuable derivatives of the central functions. The first derivative is the agency of the press in *public education*. A second is serving as a *critical forum* for analysis, disputation, and comment, in which different opinions and ideas are discussed, debated, and have it out. An idealized conception of this is attributed to the American playwright Arthur Miller: 'A good newspaper, I suppose, is a nation talking to itself'[30]. A third derivative is *agenda building*. Socially conscious media can trigger agenda-building processes to help produce democratic and progressive outcomes; and this they can do best when an authentic public opinion and a congenial context of attitude, feeling, and critical democratic values and practice exist. All this suggests that while investigation is a core function of journalism, it gains traction and power only in concert with the other functions.

When you take a wide-angle view of journalism that sees investigation as one of its intrinsic and core tasks, rather than a super-speciality or a sequestered discipline, a vast and promising vista opens of work that is truth-seeking, richly themed, exploratory, imaginative, literary, and, above all, passionate about freedom, humanity, and justice. Taking the wide-angle approach to journalism means that a much larger pool of journalists, educated and trained in the precepts and practice of quality journalism, can be drawn into the task of investigation than current professional practice allows. Motivating and empowering this greatly enlarged pool of young women and men to do thorough, thoughtful, and carefully supervised investigations into subjects of social significance, including corruption, could have dramatic effects in terms of developing capabilities, improving work culture, and raising quality in the profession.

What needs emphasis is this. While investigating, exploring, and experimenting, journalists of the first rank are not satisfied with bringing to light a mass of facts relating to corruption or abuse of power that they manage to unearth through diligent work, or that falls into their lap by a stroke of luck. Their real pursuit is to invest these hitherto concealed or inaccessible facts with social and, often, historical meaning and weave them into a coherent and compelling story, so that their journalism contributes significantly to raising social awareness of the issues involved and stands the test of time.

This is what journalism at its best can do for the fight against corruption. Nothing less must be demanded from India's journalists.

9. *Political education and mobilization is the key*: Progress in the fight against corruption does not depend mainly on laws or even their enforcement. The rule of law, while necessary, is an insufficient condition for the prevention and elimination of corruption in any society. But this is so especially in an unequal, unjust, and exploitative system of political economy where the lines between corruption and other, often legal, ways of conning, gypping, and ripping off ordinary folk, and especially the poor, the illiterate, the socially oppressed, the least socially networked, and the landless are blurred. Global anti-corruption movements and NGOs tend to project transparency, access to information, community-based efforts, and new technology as magic bullets against corruption. These can help, as we saw above, but as Sukhtankar and Vaishnav note, 'there is very little evidence to support the idea that greater transparency, information, and community-based efforts have a significant impact on reducing corruption on their own'[31]. The researchers add that the same negative finding holds true for some technological interventions, although 'those interventions that…bypass middlemen and corrupt officials have a much greater scope for success, as do interventions that transfer bargaining power to citizens and beneficiaries[32].

In fashioning a differentiated and sequenced anti-corruption strategy and putting it to work, the limitations imposed by the system of political economy and social, cultural, and historical factors must be constantly borne in mind; otherwise demoralization and defections from the movement might quickly set in. Consider, for example, the recent developments in liberalizing and incentivizing opaque corporate funding of political parties, which I have discussed in some detail in this chapter. We know that in the prevailing political situation, these regressive trends are not going to get reversed and therefore the prospects for reforming and cleansing electoral and political finance in the conceivable future are dim. But this does not mean that opposition to these trends should be at a standstill on a Micawberish expectation that 'something will turn up'.

Amartya Sen reminds us that there are different ways in which 'injustice, inequality, poverty, hunger, tyranny, ignorance, exclusion, exploitation…[and] corruption and misuse of power' can be opposed even when the prospect of mobilizing large numbers of people for direct action on these issues appears bleak:

> We have reason enough to be determined and resolute in fighting them. Such fights cannot escape being, in many ways, rather grim, since there are hard barriers to overcome. The bleakness of such fights also relates to the fact that we have to combat, often enough, forces that may be fiercely opposed to the necessary changes that can eradicate these

> intolerable phenomena... Gentle undermining can indeed be an effective means of combat.[33]
>
> The examples Sen cites include the appearance of the radical social activist Jerry Rubin and his 'co-conspirators' in fancy dress before the House Un-American Activities Committee to undermine the dignity of the paranoid witch-hunt led by Senator Joseph McCarthy; Charlie Chaplin's peerless critical comedy; and the weapon of discontent-creating literary ridicule deployed against corruption and misuse of power in ancient Indian plays like Bhasa's *Daridracharudatta* and Shudraka's *Mrichchhakatika*.

In the final analysis, progress in the fight against corruption depends on the quality and effectiveness of political education, organization, and mass mobilization—and the capacity of progressive mass-based politics to project and target corruption not as a pathological condition, but as an integral part of an unjust and exploitative system of political economy that needs to be transformed. In short, the struggle against corruption needs to be waged in parallel with a larger democratic and progressive political struggle.

There is simply no way of predicting how long it will take before significant positive gains, not to mention a radical breakthrough, can be achieved by these struggles. But it would be irresponsible for citizens to stand aside and let the hugely damaging current situation and the trends discussed in this book continue to take their toll.

ACKNOWLEDGEMENTS

C. P. Chandrasekhar, Judith Heyer, T. Jayaraman, Prakash Karat, Kanta Murali, N. S. Nigam, Vijay Prashad, and Madhura Swaminathan provided suggestions, comments, criticisms, and references during the course of my thinking about and writing this book. Colleagues at *The Hindu* and *Frontline*, especially T. Ramakrishnan, R. Vijaya Sankar, and V. Ganesan, helped me with leads and background and archival material on corruption. Ilangovan Rajasekaran of *Frontline* made a special contribution by discovering and providing unpublished documents and hard-to-access information on Tamil Nadu's granite quarrying and sand mining scandals. David Davidar, my publisher, came up with the idea of this book, including its title, and offered several suggestions while the work was in progress. Aienla Ozukum took this book through a thorough and fast editing process without my having to raise a sweat. My wife, Mariam Ram, a meticulous reader, took time off her business commitments to look out for errors, unclear passages, and infelicities that might have crept into the manuscript ahead of the final editing. I am grateful to all of them. And finally, a disclaimer: none of them is responsible for the views expressed and the arguments made in this book.

NOTES AND REFERENCES

INTRODUCTION

1. 'What is corruption?', Transparency International, http://www.transparency.org/what-is-corruption/#what-is-transparency
2. Herman Melville, *The Confidence-Man* (originally published in 1857), New York: Simon & Brown, 2016.
3. 'Herman Melville's 'The Confidence-Man', a post at Columbia University's website, http://www.columbia.edu/~lnp3/mydocs/culture/confidence_man.htm. See also John Updike, 'The Artist and His Audience', The *New York Review of Books*, 18 July 1985.
4. Christopher Daly, 'It's a scam! (History and origin of the word 'scam')', The Better Editor, 25 May 2012, https://thebettereditor.wordpress.com/2012/05/25/its-a-scam-history-and-origin-of-the-word-scam/
5. Today, the story might well originate from a hacker or a new kind of global player like WikiLeaks, https://wikileaks.org/What-is-Wikileaks.html, which describes itself as 'a multi-national media organisation and associated library' specializing in 'the analysis and publication of large datasets of censored or otherwise restricted materials involving war, spying and corruption.'
6. In his pioneering study, *India's Newspaper Revolution*, Robin Jeffrey remarks that 'immense curiosity built up…inside the bottle into which Mrs Gandhi had jammed a cork in 1975… The immense curiosity…generated a market for anyone with a story to tell

and a press to print it on.' Jeffrey's study shows how political, technological, and economic circumstances had come together in the late 1970s to create India's 'newspaper revolution'. See Robin Jeffrey, *India's Newspaper Revolution: Capitalism, Politics and the Indian-language Press 1977-99,* New Delhi: Oxford University Press, 2000, pp. 18, 38-39.

7. Upendra Baxi, *Liberty and Corruption: The Antulay Case and Beyond*, Lucknow: Eastern Book Company, 1989, p. 7.

8. Melvin Mencher, *News Reporting and Writing*, Eighth Edition, New York: McGraw-Hill Higher Education, 2000, pp. 268, 278, 284, 289-290.

9. Georg Wilhelm Friedrich Hegel, *The Philosophy of History*, originally published in the 1820s, trans. J. Sibree, Scotts Valley, California: Information Age Publishing, 2010.

10. Narendra Modi, 'PM's address to the Nation,' midnight of 8 November 2016, http://www.pmindia.gov.in/en/news_updates/ prime-ministers-address-to-the-nation/?comment=disable

11. P. Chidambaram, 'Will India Script an Uninterrupted Growth Story?', First Annual Lecture of The Hindu Centre for Politics and Public Policy, Chennai, 2017, http://www.thehinducentre. com/the-arena/current-issues/article9585211.ece

12. Arun Kumar, *Understanding the Black Economy and Black Money in India: An Enquiry into Causes, Consequences and Remedies*, New Delhi: Aleph Book Company, 2017; Jayati Ghosh, C. P. Chandrasekhar, and Prabhat Patnaik, *Demonetisation Decoded: A Critique of India's Currency Experiment*, London & New York: Routledge, 2017; and C. Rammanohar Reddy, *Demonetisation and Black Money*, with a Foreword by Y. V. Reddy, Hyderabad: Orient Black Swan, 2017.

13. Supreme Court of India, judgment of two-member bench comprising Justices Pinaki Chandra Ghose and Amitava Roy in 'Criminal Appeal Nos 300-303 of 2017, State of Karnataka, appellants vs Selvi J. Jayalalithaa & ors, respondents', etc., http:// supremecourtofindia.nic.in/FileServer/2017-02-14_1487056122. pdf

14. In this shortlist of living political leaders, only Lalu Prasad has been convicted by a trial court and consequently disqualified for membership of parliament or a state legislature, even though he

remains active and powerful as the unchallenged leader of a major regional party. In 2006, both Lalu Prasad and his wife, former Chief Minister Rabri Devi, were acquitted by a CBI court in a disproportionate assets case registered in 1998. In 2013, he was found guilty of embezzlement in a 1990s case known as the 'fodder scam', appealed against his conviction and sentence, and was subsequently released on bail by order of the Supreme Court. The other leaders named in the shortlist have faced legal proceedings that have not yet been finally adjudicated. Former chief minister and BJP leader Yeddyurappa won relief from the judiciary, which quashed several criminal charges against him for want of evidence.

ONE: CORRUPTION AND SCAMS AS MOST INDIANS KNOW THEM

1. The term 'folklore of corruption' seems to have been coined by Gunnar Myrdal, the Nobel Prize-winning Swedish economist. If he did not invent it, he certainly brought it into vogue. See Gunnar Myrdal, 'Corruption: Its Causes and Effects', *Asian Drama: An Inquiry into the Poverty of Nations*, New York: The Twentieth Century Fund, 1968, vol II, chapter 20, pp. 937-960.
2. Nicholas B. Dirks, *The Scandal of Empire: India and the Creation of Imperial Britain*, Cambridge, Massachusetts & London: Harvard University Press, 2006, p. 57.
3. Charles Cornwallis, 'Earl Cornwallis to the Right Hon. Henry Dundas, 14 August 1787', private letter published in *Correspondence of Charles, First Marquis Cornwallis*, edited with notes by Charles Ross, Esq., in three volumes, Second Edition, vol. I, London: John Murray, Albemarle Street, 1859, p. 282. The original volume, which is with the New York Public Library, was digitized by Google, https://babel.hathitrust.org/cgi/pt?id=nyp.33433081650933;view=1up;seq=15
4. Edmund Burke, 'Speech in General Reply,' 5 June 1794, in the Impeachment of Warren Hastings, *The Works of The Right Honourable Edmund Burke In Twelve Volumes*, Volume the Eleventh,

London: John C. Nimmo. The downloadable pdf file has been placed in the public domain by McMaster University, p. 209, http://socserv2.socsci.mcmaster.ca/econ/ugcm/3ll3/burke/Works11.pdf
5. Santhanam Committee, *Report of The Committee on Prevention of Corruption*, Ministry of Home Affairs, Government of India, New Delhi, 1964, digitized copy, pp. 5, 11-12.
6. Gunnar Myrdal, *Asian Drama: An Inquiry into the Poverty of Nations*, pp. 937-960.
7. Upendra Baxi, *Liberty and Corruption*, p. 170.
8. Pranab Bardhan, *Globalisation, Democracy and Corruption*, Kolkata: Frontpage, 2015, p. 91.
9. Gunnar Myrdal, *Asian Drama: An Inquiry into the Poverty of Nations*, p. 941.
10. Akhil Gupta, *Red Tape: Bureaucracy, Structural Violence, and Poverty in India*, A John Hope Franklin Center Book, Durham & London: Duke University Press, 2012, pp. 75-138.
11. Gunnar Myrdal, *Asian Drama: An Inquiry into the Poverty of Nations*, pp. 939-958.
12. Sandip Sukhtankar and Milan Vaishnav, 'Corruption in India: Bridging Research Evidence and Policy Options', paper presented at the India Policy Forum, 2015, Table 1, with details in Appendix A.
13. On the face of it, ₹50 crore was a real bargain for the bribers to ensure the survival of the minority government. But the exposed bribes might have been only a small part of the corruption involved in the 2008 Cash-for-Votes scandal.
14. C. P. Chandrasekhar, 'Age of Graft', *Frontline*, 31 May 2013, p. 13.

TWO: THE MULTIFARIOUSNESS OF CORRUPTION

1. Pranab Bardhan, 'Corruption and Development: A Review of Issues', *Journal of Economic Literature*, 1997, vol. 35, 3, pp. 1320–1346.
2. Arun Kumar, *Understanding the Black Economy and Black Money in India*, p. xv.
3. Ibid. p. x
4. Joe Roeber, *Parallel Markets: Corruption in the International Arms*

Trade, text of Campaign Against Arms Trade lecture at the London School of Economics, 2005.

5. SIPRI (Stockholm International Peace Research Institute), 'Fact Sheet: Trends in World Military Expenditure, 2015', 2016, http://books.sipri.org/files/FS/SIPRIFS1604.pdf

6. Debashis Basu and Sucheta Dalal, *The Scam: From Harshad Mehta to Ketan Parekh*, Mumbai: KenSource Information Services P. Ltd., 2014, p. 382.

7. 'Corporate fraud reports a 45 per cent increase in India: ASSOCHAM-Grant Thornton', news release by ASSOCHAM, http://www.assocham.org/newsdetail.php?id=4837
The survey report 'Fraud: A key governance risk', Grant Thornton and ASSOCHAM, 2014 is available at http://gtw3.grantthornton.in/assets/Grant_Thortnon_Assocham_Fraud-A_key_governance_risk.pdf

8. *Global Fraud Report: Vulnerabilities on the Rise*, Kroll, Annual Edition 2015/2016, pp. 54-55, http://anticorruzione.eu/wpcontent/uploads/2015/09/Kroll_Global_Fraud_Report_2015low-copia.pdf

9. Career progression takes precedence over ethical behaviour in corporate India: EY report', EY news release, Mumbai, 10 April 2017. The survey report is available at http://www.ey.com/Publication/vwLUAssets/EY_-_EMEIA_Fraud_Survey_2017/$FILE/ey-emeia-fraud-survey-2017.pdf

10. 'Rs 30,000 crore to be spent on Lok Sabha polls', PTI report published in the *Times of India*, 16 March 2004, http://timesofindia.indiatimes.com/general-elections-2014/more-stories/Rs-30000-crore-to-be-spent-on-Lok-Sabha polls/articleshow/32138176.cms?utm_source=twitter.com&utm_medium=referral&utm_campaign=timesofindia/

11. 'Elections in last five years cost Rs 1.5 lakh crore: Study', report in the *Economic Times*, 23 April 2014, http://economictimes.indiatimes.com/news/politics-and-nation/elections-in-last-five-years-cost-rs-1-5-lakh-crore-study/articleshow/34106356.cms

12. A. P. Mukherjee, *Unknown Facets of Rajiv Gandhi, Jyoti Basu, Indrajit Gupta*, New Delhi: Manas Publications, 2014, pp. 90-91.

13. Milan Vaishnav, *When Crime Pays: Money and Muscle in Indian Politics*,

New Delhi: HarperCollins Publishers India, 2017, pp. 54-69.
14. Pranab Bardhan, 'The economist's approach to the problem of corruption', *World Development*, vol. 34, 2 February 2006, pp. 341.
15. Mehul Srivastava and Andrew Macaskill, 'India's Poor Starve as Politicians Steal Their Food: Investigations of massive food scams have gone on for years, but there have been no convictions', *Bloomberg*, 7 September 2012, https://www.bloomberg.com/news/articles/2012-09-06/indias-poor-starve-as-politicians-steal-their-food
16. Ibid.
17. Ibid.
18. Ibid.
19. Paul R. Brass, *An Indian Political Life: Charan Singh and Congress Politics, 1937 to 1961*, New Delhi: Sage Publications, 2011, p. 158.
20. Pranab Bardhan, *Globalisation, Democracy and Corruption*, p. 90.
21. Shylashri Shankar and Raghav Gaija, *Battling Corruption: Has NREGA Reached India's Rural Poor?*, New Delhi: Oxford University Press, 2013.
22. P. Sainath, 'Paid News will wipe out journalism', interview *Pragati*, 10 June 2010, https://groups.google.com/forum/#!msg/progressive-interactions/-tXD9EFD18w/zQX11IQN1iAJ
23. Press Council of India, 'Sub-Committee Report on "Paid News": How corruption in the Indian media undermines democracy', 7 October 2009, http://presscouncil.nic.in/OldWebsite/Sub-CommitteeReport.pdf. The sub-committee's report, submitted in 2009, was officially withheld for two years and uploaded at the PCI's website in compliance with a direction from the Central Information Commission.
24. 'Report on Paid News', Press Council of India, 30 July 2010, http://presscouncil.nic.in/OldWebsite/CouncilReport.pdf
25. N. Ram, 'The Changing Role of the News Media in Contemporary India', address as president of the Contemporary India section of the Indian History Congress, 72nd Session, Patiala, 10 December 2011, https://pdfs.semanticscholar.org/9b3a/f690a7c3186fca407e38c6a198677afaa5f3.pdf

THREE: LAW AND ENFORCEMENT

1. Upendra Baxi, *Liberty and Corruption*, pp. 2, 162.
2. The Prevention of Corruption Act 1988, http://lawmin.nic.in/ld/P-ACT/1988/The%20Prevention%20of%20Corruption%20Act,%201988.pdf
3. Law Commission of India, 'Report No. 254 of the Law Commission of India, on The Prevention of Corruption (Amendment) Bill 2013', February 2015, http://lawcommissionofindia.nic.in/reports/Report_No.254_Prevention_of_Corruption.pdf
4. See 'Table 3: Provisions of the UN Convention that are not covered in the Bill', in the PRS Legislative Brief on the Prevention of Corruption (Amendment) Bill 2013, http://www.prsindia.org/uploads/media/Corruption/Legislative%20Brief-%20Prevention%20of%20Corruption%20%28Amendment%29%20Bill%202013.pdf
5. PRS Legislative Brief on the Prevention of Corruption (Amendment) Bill 2013.
6. The Whistleblower Protection Act 2011 (Act No. 17 of 2014), http://www.indiacode.nic.in/acts2014/17%20of%202014.pdf
7. The Official Secrets Act 1923, http://www.archive.india.gov.in/allimpfrms/allacts/3314.pdf
8. Right to Information Act 2005, http://rti.gov.in/rti-act.pdf
9. PRS Legislative Brief, The Whistleblowers Protection (Amendment) Bill 2015, http://www.prsindia.org/uploads/media/Public%20Disclosure/Brief%20Whistleblowers%20Protection%20(Amendment)%20Bill%202015.pdf
10. The Lokpal and Lokayuktas Act 2013, http://www.indiacode.nic.in/acts2014/1%20of%202014.pdf
11. Email of 7 March 2017 from N. S. Nigam to N. Ram.
12. Sandip Sukhtankar and Milan Vaishnav, 'Corruption in India', pp. 5, 8, 9.
13. Ibid, pp. 8-9
14. CHRI (Commonwealth Human Rights Initiative), 'Fact and Fiction: Governments' Efforts to Combat Corruption: CHRI's Preliminary findings from a study of NCRB's Statistics (2001-

2015)', 2016, http://www.humanrightsinitiative.org/download/CHRI-IndiaCorruptionstats.pdf

FOUR: 'ASIATIC CORRUPTION' AND THE SCANDAL OF EMPIRE

1. Pranab Bardhan, 'The Economist's Approach to the Problem of Corruption', p. 344.
2. Nicholas B. Dirks, *The Scandal of Empire,* p. 17.
3. Ibid, p. 13
4. Peter Bratsis, 'Political Corruption Under Transnational Capitalism: A Marxist View', *The Marxist*, July-September 2014, pp. 3-22.
5. 'Corruption Perceptions Index 2016', Transparency International, http://www.transparency.org/news/feature/corruption_perceptions_index_2016
6. Transparency International maintains that 'there is no meaningful way to assess absolute levels of corruption in countries or territories on the basis of hard empirical data'. Data and Methodology, http://www.transparency.org/cpi2015#downloads
7. See, for instance, Bratsis, 'Political Corruption Under Transnational Capitalism'.
8. The Bribe Payers Index 2011, http://www.transparency.org/whatwedo/publication/bpi_2011
9. Josy Joseph, *A Feast of Vultures: The Hidden Business of Democracy in India*, New Delhi: HarperCollins Publishers India, 2016, p. 60.
10. UK Bribery Act 2010, http://www.legislation.gov.uk/ukpga/2010/23/pdfs/ukpga_20100023_en.pdf
11. BAE Systems Case (2008, 2010), 'BAE paid too little heed to ethics, says report', Sadie Gray, David Leigh, and Rob Evans, *The Guardian*, 6 May 2008, https://www.theguardian.com/business/2008/may/06/baesystemsbusiness.armstrade;

    'BAE admits guilt over corrupt arms deals', David Leigh and Rob Evans, *The Guardian*, 6 February 2010, https://www.theguardian.com/world/2010/feb/05/bae-systems-arms-deal-corruption;

    'Settlement of BAE Systems Corruption Cases: significant issues of concern', Note by Transparency International UK, 11 February

2010, https://www.transparency.org.uk/wp-content/plugins/download-attachments/includes/download.php?id=1020;

'BAE Systems: timeline of bribery allegations', *The Telegraph*, 21 December 2010, http://www.telegraph.co.uk/finance/newsbysector/industry/defence/8216172/BAE-Systems-timeline-of-bribery-allegations.html

12. Rolls-Royce Case (2017), 'SFO completes £497.25m Deferred Prosecution Agreement with Rolls-Royce PLC', Serious Fraud Office news release, 17 January 2017, https://www.sfo.gov.uk/2017/01/17/sfo-completes-497-25m-deferred-prosecution-agreement-rolls-royce-plc/;

'SFO–v-Rolls-Royce judgment—Courts and Tribunals Judiciary', https://www.judiciary.gov.uk/wp-content/uploads/2017/01/sfo-v-rolls-royce.pdf

'Rolls-Royce to pay £671 million over bribery claims', Rob Evans, David Pegg, and Holly Watt, *The Guardian*, 16 January 2017, https://www.theguardian.com/business/2017/jan/16/rolls-royce-to-pay-671m-over-bribery-claims

'Rolls-Royce apologises in court after settling bribery case', Holly Watt, David Pegg, and Rob Evans, *The Guardian*, 17 January 2017, https://www.theguardian.com/business/2017/jan/17/rolls-royce-apologises-bribery-671m-uk-us-brazil

'Did Rolls-Royce get off lightly over "truly vast" bribery?', Alan Tovey, *The Telegraph*, 17 January 2017, http://www.telegraph.co.uk/business/2017/01/17/did-rolls-royce-get-lightly-truly-vast-bribery/

'Rolls-Royce—Cooperation not confession unlocks 50% DPA discount', Tony Lewis, Alexandra Underwood, and Natalia Quinlivan, *Fieldfisher*, 18 January 2017, http://www.fieldfisher.com/publications/2017/01/rolls-royce-cooperation-not-confession-unlocks-50-dpa-discount#sthash.nbkWo22d.dpbs

'Rolls-Royce—cooperation not confession unlocks DPA', Alexandra Underwood, *Fieldfisher*, 9 February 2017, http://www.fieldfisher.com/publications/2017/02/rolls-royce-cooperation-not-confession-unlocks-dpa#sthash.SLWaoYz5.dpbs

'File criminal case against Rolls-Royce', Special Correspondent, *The Hindu*, 21 March 2017, http://www.thehindu.com/news/

national/file-criminal-case-against-rolls-royce/article17547662. ece

13. Cognizant reported that it was 'conducting an internal investigation into whether certain payments relating to facilities in India were made improperly and in possible violation of the US Foreign Corrupt Practices Act and other applicable laws', that it had 'voluntarily notified' the US Department of Justice and the SEC, and that it was 'cooperating fully with both agencies', *Report of unscheduled material events, or corporate changes*, Item 8.0.1 of regulatory filing by Cognizant Technology Solutions Corp. on 30 September 2016, http://investors.cognizant.com/filings

14. 'Annual report with a comprehensive overview of the company', filed with the SEC on 1 March 2017 for the fiscal year ending 31 December 2016, http://investors.cognizant.com/filings.

15. 'File criminal case against Rolls-Royce', report by Special Correspondent in *The Hindu*, 21 March 2017, http://www.thehindu.com/news/national/file-criminal-case-against-rolls-royce/article17547662.ece

FIVE: CONCEPTUALIZING AND DEFINING CORRUPTION

1. Pranab Bardhan, 'The Economist's Approach to the Problem of Corruption', p. 341.
2. Pranab Bardhan, 'Corruption and Development', p. 1321.
3. See, for instance, Nico Groenendijk, 'A principal-agent model of corruption', *Crime Law and Social Change*, April 1997, pp. 207-229, https://www.researchgate.net/publication/225852596_A_principal-agent_model_of_corruption
4. Gordon Tulloch, 'The Welfare Costs of Tariffs, Monopolies, and Theft', *Western Economic Journal*, 5:3, June 1967, pp. 224-232, http://cameroneconomics.com/tullock%201967.pdf
5. Toke S. Aidt, 'Rent seeking and the economics of corruption', *Constitutional Political Economy*, vol. 27, 2 June 2016, pp. 142-157.
6. Pranab Bardhan, 'Corruption and Development', p. 1339.
7. Irene Hors, 'Rent-Seeking Behaviour and Public Corruption', paper presented at the 8th International Anti-Corruption

Conference, Lima, Peru, September 1997, http://www.8iacc.org/papers/ihors.html
8. UN Anti-Corruption Tool-kit UNEP, Chapter 1: Introduction, http://www.pogar.org/publications/finances/anticor/anticorruptiontoolkit.pdf
9. *United Nations Convention Against Corruption*, with Foreword by Secretary General Kofi A. Annan, https://www.unodc.org/documents/brussels/UN_Convention_Against_Corruption.pdf

SIX: POLITICAL CORRUPTION THROUGH A MARXIST LENS

1. Prakash Karat, 'The Political Economy of Corruption', *The Marxist*, July-September 2011, 3, pp. 19-20.
2. Robert Mayer, 'Marx, Lenin and the Corruption of the Working Class', *Political Studies*, XLI, 1993, p. 636, http://www.aibsnleatn.com/current_events/mayer4.pdf
3. Ibid, pp. 641-648.
4. Peter Bratsis, 'Political Corruption Under Transnational Capitalism', pp. 3-4.
5. Prakash Karat, 'The Political Economy of Corruption', p. 24.
6. Louis Althusser, et. al., *Reading Capital: The Complete Edition*, trans. Ben Brewster and David Fernbach, 2015, p. 42.
7. Louis Althusser, *For Marx*, trans. Ben Brewster, London: Allen Lane, originally published in French as *Pour Marx* in 1965, p. 152 (of the English edition).
8. Peter Bratsis, 'Political Corruption Under Transnational Capitalism', p. 4.
9. Prakash Karat, 'The Political Economy of Corruption', p. 25.
10. Peter Bratsis, 'Political Corruption Under Transnational Capitalism', p. 21.
11. Ibid, p. 18.
12. Ibid, p. 15.
13. Pranab Bardhan, *Globalisation, Democracy and Corruption*, pp. 89-90.
14. Kanta Murali, *Caste, Class, and Capital: The Social and Political Origins of Economic Policy in India*, Cambridge: Cambridge University Press, 2017, pp. 249-250.

15. Crony capitalism is usually defined as an economy in which business growth and success are enabled by close relations between business entities and the state. *The Economist* (2016), which has published an updated crony-capitalism index, a handy if oversimplified exercise, describes crony capitalists as 'individuals who earn their riches thanks to their chumminess with government'. It lists ten 'rent-seeking' or 'crony' business sectors, which because 'they have a lot of interaction with the state are vulnerable to crony capitalism'. In 2016 India ranked ninth in *The Economist*'s crony-capitalism index, with Turkey, Indonesia, Mexico, Ukraine, Singapore, Philippines, Malaysia, and Russia faring worse.
16. Prakash Karat, 'The Political Economy of Corruption', p. 20.
17. C. P. Chandrasekhar, 'Age of Graft', p. 13.
18. Peter Bratsis comments that 'there has yet to emerge a systemic or cohesive Marxist understanding of political corruption as such', 'Political Corruption Under Transnational Capitalism'.

SEVEN: BOFORS: THE DEFINING GRAND CORRUPTION SCANDAL

1. Henrik Westander, *Classified: The Political Cover-up of the Bofors Scandal*, trans. Saam Kapadia from the Swedish original, Bombay: Sterling Newspapers Pvt. Ltd, 1992, p. 86. The text of Magnus Nilsson's news broadcast, as translated from Swedish by Saam Kapadia, is reproduced in Westander's book.
2. Ibid, p. 137.
3. Central Intelligence Agency, 'Sweden's Bofors Arms Scandal: Diversions, Investigations, and Implications', 1988, sanitized copy of paper prepared by the West European Division, Office of European Analysis, approved for release on 27 March 2014, https://www.cia.gov/library/readingroom/docs/CIA-RDP90T00100R000300300001-7.pdf
4. Ibid.
5. Sten Lindstrom, 'The Bofors Story, 25 Years After', interview to Chitra Subramaniam Duella, *The Hoot*, 24 April 2012, http://www.thehoot.org/media-watch/media-practice/the-

bofors-story-25-years-after-5884
6. Ibid.
7. Ibid.
8. Kim Philby, *My Silent War: The Soviet Master Agent Tells His Own Story*, New York: Grove Press, Inc., 1968, p. 255.
9. Robert Southey, 'The Battle of Blenheim', written in 1798, https://www.poetryfoundation.org/poems-and-poets/poems/detail/45178
10. 'Delhi High Court quashes bribery charges in Bofors case', news report in *The Hindu*, 5 February 2004, http://www.thehindu.com/2004/02/05/stories/2004020508380100.htm
11. Srichand P. Hinduja vs State Through CBI, judgment of the Delhi High Court dated 31 May 2005, bench: Justice R. S. Sodhi, https://indiankanoon.org/doc/230231/
12. Quoted in 'Quattrocchi dies in Milan', report by Sandeep Joshi in *The Hindu*, 11 July 2013, http://www.thehindu.com/news/international/Quattrocchi-dies-in-Milan/article12004110.ece

EIGHT: TAMIL NADU'S SCIENTIFIC SYSTEM OF POLITICAL CORRUPTION

1. Professional Examination Board (PEB), 'Mission & Vision', http://www.vyapam.nic.in/e_default.html
2. The official count of these suspicious deaths is 24 but unofficial estimates range from 44 to 156. Source: 'Vyapam: How a Munnabhai-style Exam Scam Turned Into a Macabre Thriller', Rakesh Dixit, *The Wire*, 1 July 2015, https://thewire.in/5249/vyapam-how-a-munnabhai-style-exam-scam-turned-into-a-macabre-thriller/
3. Aman Sethi, 'The Mystery of India's Deadly Exam Scam', *The Guardian*, 17 December 2015, https://www.theguardian.com/world/2015/dec/17/the-mystery-of-indias-deadly-exam-scam
4. Rakesh Dixit, 'As Vyapam Goes to CBI, Hopes Rise that "DMAT Scam" Will Be Probed Too', *The Wire*, 14 July 2015, https://thewire.in/6275/as-vyapam-goes-to-cbi-hopes-rise-that-dmat-scam-will-be-probed-too/

5. 'MP's DMAT scam seems to be worse than Vyapam, Supreme Court says', Amit Anand Choudhary, *Times of India*, 17 July 2015, http://timesofindia.indiatimes.com/india/MPs-DMAT-scam-seems-to-be-worse-than-Vyapam-scam-Supreme-Court-says/articleshow/48106366.cms
6. 'MP DMAT scam bigger than Vyapam: CBI tells Supreme Court', Amit Anand Choudhary, *Times of India*, 13 August 2015, http://timesofindia.indiatimes.com/india/MP-DMAT-scam-bigger-than-Vyapam-CBI-tells-Supreme-Court/articleshow/48461145.cms
7. 'As Vyapam Goes to CBI, Hopes Rise that "DMAT Scam" Will Be Probed Too', Rakesh Dixit, *The Wire*, 14 July 2015, https://thewire.in/6275/as-vyapam-goes-to-cbi-hopes-rise-that-dmat-scam-will-be-probed-too/
8. Sandip Sukhtankar and Milan Vaishnav who propose these three categories based on the actions of public officials, define *facilitative* corruption as corruption that 'involves officials charging fees or bribes for activities that they should be doing in the first place'; *collusive* corruption as officials 'breaking or bending rules to benefit bribers'; and *extractive* corruption as officials extracting funds from the government or private parties, 'either through harassment or stealth', 'Corruption in India', pp. 14-15.
9. A fuller list of allegations of corruption against the Tamil Nadu government is available in a twenty-two-page petition presented by the Pattali Makkal Katchi (PMK) to the Governor in February 2015. The petition was referenced as 'Corruption and misuse of power by the Ministers and of Government of Tamil Nadu—request for calling a report from the Chief Minister of Tamil Nadu—demand for constituting an Enquiry Commission regarding.' Unsurprisingly, nothing came of it.
10. Ilangovan Rajasekaran, 'The mother of all loot', *Frontline*, 24 July 2015, p. 14, http://www.frontline.in/cover-story/the-mother-of-all-loot/article7391496.ece
11. M. Rajshekar, 'Politicians aren't only messing with Tamil Nadu's water—they're making ₹20,000 crore from sand', *Scroll*, 19 September 2016, https://scroll.in/article/815138/tamil-nadus-political-parties-are-making-money-from-sand-worth-a-

whopping-rs-20000-crore-a-year;
'Think sand mining damages the ecology? It ruins politics as well', 20 September 2016, https://scroll.in/article/815139/think-sand-mining-damages-the-ecology-it-ruins-politics-as-well; and 'Sand mining in Tamil Nadu is incredibly destructive—but it's also unstoppable,' 21 September 2016, https://scroll.in/article/815140/why-sand-mining-in-tamil-nadu-is-unstoppable-even-though-its-destructive

12. *Frontline*, 2015.
13. Sandhya Ravishankar, 'The Countdown Begins For Tamil Nadu's Beach Sand Mining Cartel', *The Wire,* 27 January 2017, https://thewire.in/102506/countdown-begins-tamil-nadus-beach-sand-mining-cartel/
    —'In Tamil Nadu, Sixteen Years Of Sand Mining Loot Officially Termed "Illegal"', 20 February 2017, https://thewire.in/110405/tamil-nadu-sand-mining/
14. A thirteen-page-report in Tamil, dated 5 May 2012, submitted by U. Sagayam, Madurai District Collector, to the Principal Secretary, Industries Department, Government of Tamil Nadu.
15. *Probe into Granite Mining Activities in Madurai District: Report Submitted to The Hon'ble High Court Madras* by U. Sagayam, I.A.S., Special Officer/Legal Commissioner, 23 November 2015, 624 pages.
16. Ilangovan Rajasekaran, 'Removing roadblocks', *Frontline,* 9 December 2014, p. 24, http://www.frontline.in/the-nation/removing-roadblocks/article6632957.ece
17. Executive Summary, *Probe into Granite Mining Activities in Madurai District: Report Submitted to The Hon'ble High Court Madras* by U. Sagayam, I.A.S., Special Officer/Legal Commissioner, 23 November 2015, 624 pages.
18. Ibid, p. xii.
19. Ibid, p. xiii.
20. Ibid, p. xxi.
21. Ibid, pp. xxiv-xxv.
22. Ibid, p. xxvii.
23. Andrew Wyatt, 'Populism and Politics in Contemporary Tamil Nadu', *Contemporary South Asia*, vol. 21, No. 4, 2013, pp. 365-381.

———, 'Combining Clientelist and Programmatic Politics in Tamil Nadu, South India', *Commonwealth & Comparative Politics*, vol. 51, No. 1, 2013, pp. 27-55.

24. John Harriss and Andrew Wyatt, 'Business and Politics: The Tamil Nadu Puzzle', unpublished.
25. Andrew Wyatt, *Contemporary South Asia*.
26. Andrew Wyatt, *Commonwealth & Comparative Politics*.
27. Anna Dravida Munnetra Kazhagam (ADMK) was the original name of the party that M. G. Ramachandran founded in 1972. Subsequently, in a self-conscious nod towards nationalism, it was renamed the All India Anna Dravida Munnetra Kazhagam (AIADMK).
28. I could not find a reference to the term 'scientific corruption' in any of the volumes of the Sarkaria Commission report, but it is widely quoted by secondary sources. It is possible that this description was used during a briefing to the censored press during the Emergency.
29. 'AIADMK chief Jayalalithaa's statement', 11 February 2011, http://www.ndtv.com/india-news/aiadmk-chief-jayalalithaas-statement-447506. In this statement on the DMK and the 2G Spectrum scandal issued weeks before the 2011 Tamil Nadu Assembly election, Jayalalithaa commented: 'Tamil Nadu's Chief Minister M. Karunanidhi deserves to be complimented for one thing at least. When it comes to scientific corruption, he has shown remarkable consistency right from his very first term as Chief Minister in the late 1960s'. She cited a 'small example' from Volume 1 of the Sarkaria Commission Final Reports before concluding: 'One can only sympathise with Justice Sarkaria. He had to sift such confusing data in 28 different charges! Little wonder that he certified Karunanidhi as the "Master of Scientific Corruption!"'.
30. Sarkaria Commission of Inquiry, *Final Reports*, vols. *1, 2, 3 & 4*, Madras: Government of Tamil Nadu, 1978.
31. M. S. S. Pandian, *The Image Trap: M. G. Ramachandran in Film and Politics*, New Delhi: Sage Publications, 1992, pp. 21-24.
32. See (retired Madras High Court judge) K. Chandru, 'Bottle in Your Hand, Law is Mine', *Lawyers Collective*, 30 August 2013, http://

www.lawyerscollective.org/blog/amicus-curiae/bottle-hand-law

33. TASMAC procures Indian Made Foreign Spirits from eleven distilleries, beer from seven breweries, and wine from one winery in the state, according to the 2016-2017 policy note of the Home, Prohibition and Excise Department of the Tamil Nadu government, http://cms.tn.gov.in/sites/default/files/documents/home_prohexc_e_pn_2016_17.pdf

    Cronyism has been rampant in TASMAC's procurement practices, with company documents revealing that the family of V. K. Sasikala has benefitted through Midas Golden Distilleries Private Limited being a major supplier to the state monopoly. Also see: Aam Aadmi Party, 'Crony Capitalism in Tamil Nadu', http://www.aamaadmiparty.org/crony-capitalism-in-tamil-nadu;

    Sandhya Ravishankar, 'Tamil Nadu's "corrupt" cash cow TASMAC: How politics & liquor came to form a potent mix in the state', *Economic Times*, 11 January 2015, http://economictimes.indiatimes.com/news/politics-and-nation/tamil-nadus-corrupt-cash-cow-tasmac-how-politics-liquor-came-to-form-a-potent-mix-in-the-state/articleshow/45837423.cms

34. 'High Court reserves judgment in TASMAC appointments case', news report in *The Hindu*, 6 January 2016, updated on 22 September 2016, http://www.thehindu.com/news/cities/Madurai/High-Court-reserves-judgment-in-Tasmac-appointments-case/article13983282.ece

35. M. G. Devasahayam 'The Politics of Prohibition in Tamil Nadu,' *The Wire*, 15 April 2016, https://thewire.in/29736/the-politics-of-prohibition-in-tamil-nadu/

36. 'Policy Note 2016-2017', Prohibition and Excise, Home, Prohibition and Excise Department of the Government of Tamil Nadu, pp. 24-25, http://cms.tn.gov.in/sites/default/files/documents/home_prohexc_e_pn_2016_17.pdf

37. 'Jayalalithaa government "most corrupt": Amit Shah', PTI report, *The Hindu*, 13 April 2016, http://www.thehindu.com/elections/tamilnadu2016/jayalalithaa-government-most-corrupt-amit-shah/article8471784.ece

38 V. Geetha, 'The Undemocratic Regime of Jayalalithaa: Why Claims of Amma's Feminist Legacy Must Be Viewed With Suspicion',

The Caravan, 9 December 2016, http://www.caravanmagazine.in/vantage/undemocratic-regime-jayalalithaa-claims-of-ammas-feminist-legacy-viewed-with-suspicion

39. Sangeetha Kandavel and Sanjay Vijayakumar, 'Behind cash and gold seized in Chennai IT raids, lies a tale of big contracts', *The Hindu*, 10 December 2016, http://www.thehindu.com/news/cities/chennai/Behind-cash-and-gold-seized-in-Chennai-IT-raids-lies-a-tale-of-many-big-contracts/article16786997.ece

40. Sangeetha Kandavel, 'Taxmen raid T.N. Chief Secretary,' *The Hindu*, 22 December 2016, http://www.thehindu.com/news/national/tamil-nadu/Taxmen-raid-T.N.-Chief-Secretary/article16920271.ece

41. B. Sivakumar, 'Income Tax officials raid Tamil Nadu Chief Secretary Rama Mohan Rao's residence,' *Times of India*, 21 December 2016, http://timesofindia.indiatimes.com/city/chennai/income-tax-officials-raid-tamil-nadu-chief-secretary-rama-mohan-raos-residence/articleshow/56097314.cms

42. S. Vijay Kumar, 'T.N. was not aware of CRPF deployment at Chief Secretary's house,' *The Hindu*, 21 December 2016, http://www.thehindu.com/news/national/tamil-nadu/T.N.-was-not-aware-of-CRPF-deployment-at-Chief-Secretarys-house/article16917907.ece
'Ousted TN Chief Secretary terms IT raids a 'constitutional assault', news report, *Business Line*, 27 December 2016, http://www.thehindubusinessline.com/news/national/it-raids-constitutional-assault-on-chief-secys-office-rao/article9445683.ece

43. Sangeetha Kandavel, 'IT searches reveal Rs 89 crore was distributed in R.K. Nagar', *The Hindu*, 7 April 2017, updated April 8, 2017, http://www.thehindu.com/news/national/tamil-nadu/i-t-department-raids-premises-of-tn-minister-vijayabhaskar/article17859127.ece
Bharani Vaitheesvaran, 'I-T raid in Tamil Nadu health minister Vijaya Bhaskar residence', *Economic Times*, 8 April 2017, http://economictimes.indiatimes.com/news/politics-and-nation/i-t-raid-in-tamil-nadu-health-minister-vijaya-bhaskar-residence/articleshow/58059721.cms

44. Order of the Election Commission of India, dated 9 April 2017,

in regard to the By-Election to Tamil Nadu Legislative Assembly from 11-Dr. Radhakrishnan Nagar Assembly Constituency, http://eci.nic.in/eci_main1/current/ByeElectionTN_09042017.pdf

CONCLUSION: WHAT CAN BE DONE ABOUT CORRUPTION AND SCAMS?

1. William Shakespeare, *Julius Caesar*, performed in 1599, *The Oxford Shakespeare: The Complete Works*, second edition, Oxford: Clarendon Press, 2005.
2. Sandip Sukhtankar and Milan Vaishnav, 'Corruption in India', pp. 8-9.
3. CHRI, 2016, http://www.humanrightsinitiative.org/download/CHRI-IndiaCorruptionstats.pdf
4. *Annual Report, 2016-17*, Department of Food & Public Distribution, Ministry of Consumer Affairs, Food & Public Distribution, Government of India, pp. 56-57, http://dfpd.nic.in/writereaddata/images/annual-140217.pdf
5. 'What Do the Numbers Tell? An Analysis of Union Budget 2017-18', Centre for Budget and Governance Accountability, New Delhi.
6. Harish Damodaran, 'Universal PDS model, efficient in controlling grain leakages', *Business Line*, 28 March 2011, http://www.thehindubusinessline.com/economy/universal-pds-model-efficient-in-controlling-grain-leakages/article1579499.ece
7. Himanshu and Abhijit Sen, 'In-Kind Food Transfers–I and II: Impact on Poverty,' *Economic & Political Weekly*, 16 and 23 November 2013.
8. Jean Dreze and Reetika Khera, 'Understanding leakages in the Public Distribution System', *Economic & Political Weekly*, 14 February 2015.
9. Madhura Swaminathan, *Weakening Welfare*, New Delhi: Leftword Books, 2000, pp. 103-104.
10. 'Reorient social sector subsidies: NITI Aayog', Yuthika Bhargava, *The Hindu*, 26 April 2017, http://www.thehindu.com/business/reorient-social-sector-subsidies-niti-aayog/article18226290.ece
11. Prakash Karat, 'The Political Economy of Corruption', pp. 24-25.

12. Prakash Karat, 'Political Parties Funding: Helping Big Money in Politics', *People's Democracy*, 2 April 2017, http://peoplesdemocracy.in/2017/0212_pd/political-parties-funding-helping-big-money-politics
13. Budget 2017-2018, Speech of Arun Jaitley, Minister of Finance, *Business Line*. 1 February 2017, http://www.thehindubusinessline.com/multimedia/archive/03126/BudgetSpeech_2017-_3126487a.pdf
14. Finance Act 2017, http://bombayhighcourt.nic.in/libweb/actc/yearwise/2017/2017.07.pdf
15. The Companies Act 2013, https://www.mca.gov.in/Ministry/pdf/CompaniesAct2013.pdf
16. The Income Tax Act 1961, http://www.incometaxindia.gov.in/pages/acts/income-tax-act.aspx
17. The Representation of the People Act 1951, http://lawmin.nic.in/legislative/election/volume%201/representation%20of%20the%20people%20act,%201951.pdf
18. The Reserve Bank of India Act 1934, as amended up to 27 June 2016, https://rbidocs.rbi.org.in/rdocs/Publications/PDFs/RBIA1934170510.PDF
19. Budget 2017-2018, Speech of Arun Jaitley, Minister of Finance, 1 February 2017, http://www.thehindubusinessline.com/multimedia/archive/03126/BudgetSpeech_2017-_3126487a.pdf
20. Twesh Mishra, 'Political funding to get a fillip with electoral bonds scheme', *Business Line*, 2 April 2017, http://www.thehindubusinessline.com/news/national/electoral-bonds-scheme-soon-breakfast-with-bl-and-jaitley/article9612468.ece
21. 'Jaitley bats for crowdfunding parties', *The Hindu*, 3 April 2017, http://www.thehindu.com/todays-paper/tp-national/jaitley-bats-for-crowdfunding-parties/article17764648.ece
22. 'Unlimited Corporate Funding: Subversion of Democracy,' editorial in *People's Democracy*, 2 April 2017, http://peoplesdemocracy.in/2017/0402_pd/unlimited-corporate-funding-subversion-democracy
23. '4 technologies helping us to fight corruption', Lauren Silveira, Project Specialist, Partnering Against Corruption Initiative, World Economic Forum, https://www.weforum.org/agenda/2016/04/4-

technologies-helping-us-to-fight-corruption/
24. Ibid.
25. 'Comparing crony capitalism around the world: The Economist's crony-capitalism index', *The Economist*, 5 May 2016, http://www.economist.com/blogs/graphicdetail/2016/05/daily-chart-2
26. Sandip Sukhtankar and Milan Vaishnav, 'Corruption in India', Table 1, Appendix A.
27. ICIJ (International Consortium of Investigative Journalists), 'The Panama Papers', 2016, https://panamapapers.icij.org/video/
28. 'Twelve Months of Investigations, Impact and Outrage', ICIJ, The Panama Papers, 2017, https://panamapapers.icij.org/20170403-anniversary-fundraising-campaign.html
29. Rita Sarin, 'Panama Papers: 415 Indians under scanner as probe widens,' *Indian Express*, 15 November 2016, http://indianexpress.com/article/india/india-news-india/panama-papers-black-money-tax-evasion-indians-in-the-list-4375963/
30. Arthur Miller, quoted in 'Who killed the newspaper?', *The Economist*, 24 August 2006, http://www.economist.com/node/7830218
31. Sandip Sukhtankar and Milan Vaishnav, 'Corruption in India', p.1
32. Ibid.
33. Amartya Sen, *The Country of First Boys*, eds. Antara Dev Sen and Pratik Kanjilal, New Delhi: Oxford University Press, pp. 29-34.

BIBLIOGRAPHY

Aidt, Toke S., 'Rent seeking and the economics of corruption', *Constitutional Political Economy*, vol. 27, 2 June 2016.

Althusser, Louis, *For Marx*, trans. Ben Brewster (originally published in French as *Pour Marx* by François Maspero, S. A., Paris, in 1965), London: Allen Lane, 1969.

Althusser, Louis, et. al., *Reading Capital: The Complete Edition*, trans. Ben Brewster and David Fernbach (originally published in French as *Lire le Capital* by François Maspero in 1965), London & New York: Verso, 2015.

Bardhan, Pranab, 'Corruption and Development: A Review of Issues', *Journal of Economic Literature*, vol. 35, 3, 1997.

———'The economist's approach to the problem of corruption', *World Development*, February 2006, vol. 34, 2, 2006.

———*Globalisation, Democracy and Corruption*, Kolkata: Frontpage, 2015.

Basu, Debashis and Dalal, Sucheta, *Scam: Who Won, Who Lost, Who Got Away*, New Delhi: UBS Publishers' Distributors Ltd., 1993.

———*The Scam: From Harshad Mehta to Ketan Parekh*, Mumbai: KenSource Information Services P. Ltd., 2014.

Baxi, Upendra, *Liberty and Corruption: The Antulay Case and Beyond*, Lucknow: Eastern Book Company, 1989.

Bhushan, Prashant, *Bofors: The Selling of a Nation*, New Delhi: Vision Books Pvt. Ltd., 1990.

Brass, Paul R., *An Indian Political Life: Charan Singh and Congress Politics, 1937 to 1961*, New Delhi: Sage Publications, 2011.

———*An Indian Political Life: Charan Singh and Congress Politics, 1957* to 1967, New Delhi: Sage Publications, 2012.

———*An Indian Political Life: Charan Singh and Congress Politics, 1967-1987*, New Delhi: Sage Publications, 2014.

Bratsis, Peter, 'Political Corruption Under Transnational Capitalism: A Marxist View', *The Marxist*, July-September 2014.

Brioschi, Carlo Alberto, *Corruption: A Short History*, trans. from the Italian by Antony Shugaar, Washington, DC: Brookings Institution Press, 2017.

Bull, Malcolm, 'Tumult and Corruption: Softening Up The State', *New Left Review*, July-August 2016.

Burke, Edmund, 'Speech in General Reply', in the Impeachment of Warren Hastings, *The Works of The Right Honourable Edmund Burke In Twelve Volumes*, Volume the Eleventh, London: John C. Nimmo, downloadable pdf file placed in the public domain by McMaster University, 5 June 1794.

Cameron, James, *An Indian Summer: A Personal Experience of India*, (London: Macmillan, 1974), London: Penguin Books, 1987.

Central Intelligence Agency, 'Sweden's Bofors Arms Scandal: Diversions, Investigations, and Implications', sanitised copy of paper prepared in 1988 by the West European Division, Office of European Analysis, approved for release on 27 March 2014.

Chandrasekhar, C. P., 'Age of Graft', *Frontline*, 31 May 2013.

Chidambaram, P., 'Will India Script an Uninterrupted Growth Story?', First Annual Lecture of The Hindu Centre for Politics and Public Policy, Chennai, 2017.

Commonwealth Human Rights Initiative (CHRI), 'Fact and Fiction: Governments' Efforts to Combat Corruption: CHRI's Preliminary findings from a study of NCRB's Statistics (2001-2015)', New Delhi, 2016.

Cornwallis, Charles, 'Earl Cornwallis to the Right Hon. Henry Dundas, August 14, 1787', private letter, published in *Correspondence of Charles, First Marquis Cornwallis*, edited with notes by Charles Ross, Esq., in three volumes, vol. I, London: John Murray, Albemarle Street, 1859.

Corruption Perceptions Index, Transparency International: series from 1995 to 2016.

Dirks, Nicholas B., *The Scandal of Empire: India and the Creation of Imperial Britain*, Cambridge, Mass. & London: Harvard University Press, 2006.

Drèze, Jean and Sen, Amartya, *Hunger and Public Action*, Oxford: Clarendon Press, 1989.

———ed., *Indian Development: Selected Regional Perspectives*, New Delhi: Oxford University Press, 1997.

———*India: Economic Development and Social Opportunity*, New Delhi: Oxford University Press, 1998.

Economist, The, 'Comparing crony capitalism around the world: The Economist's crony-capitalism index', 5 May 2016.

Gerring, John and Thacker, Strom C. (Winter 2005), 'Do Neoliberal Policies Deter Political Corruption?', *International Organization*, vol. 59, 1, Winter 2005.

Ghosh, Jayati, Chandrasekhar, C.P., and Patnaik, Prabhat, *Demonetisation Decoded: A Critique of India's Currency Experiment*, London & New York: Routledge, 2017.

Gramsci, Antonio, *Selections from the Prison Notebooks of Antonio Gramsci, 1929-1935*, ed. and trans. by Quentin Hoare and Geoffrey Nowell Smith, New York: International Publishers & London: Lawrence & Wishart, 1971.

Gupta, Akhil, *Red Tape: Bureaucracy, Structural Violence, and Poverty in India*, a John Hope Franklin Center Book, Durham & London: Duke University Press, 2012.

Harriss, John and Wyatt, Andrew, 'Business and Politics: The Tamil Nadu Puzzle', unpublished.

Hegel, Georg Wilhelm Friedrich, *The Philosophy of History*, written in the 1820s, trans. J. Sibree, Scotts Valley, California: Information Age Publishing, 2010.

Hors, Irene, 'Rent-Seeking Behaviour and Public Corruption', paper presented at the 8th International Anti-Corruption Conference, Lima, Peru, 1997.

International Consortium of Investigative Journalists (ICIJ), 'The Panama Papers', 2016.

Jeffrey, Robin, *India's Newspaper Revolution: Capitalism, Politics and the Indian-language Press 1977-99*, New Delhi: Oxford University Press, 2000.

Joseph, Josy, *A Feast of Vultures: The Hidden Business of Democracy in India*, New Delhi: HarperCollins Publishers India, 2016.

Karat, Prakash, 'The Political Economy of Corruption', *The Marxist*, July-September, 2011.

———'Political Parties Funding: Helping Big Money in Politics', *People's Democracy*, 2 April 2017.

Kautilya (Mauryan to post-Mauryan period), *The Arthashastra*, edited, rearranged, translated, and introduced by L. N. Rangarajan, English edition, New Delhi: Penguin Books, 1993.

Kebschull, Harvey G., 'Making It the "Significant Other" in Political Studies', *Political Science and Politics*, vol. 25, 4 December 1992.

Kejriwal, Arvind, *Swaraj*, New Delhi: HarperCollins Publishers India, 2014.

Krueger, Anne O., 'The Political Economy of the Rent-Seeking Society', *American Economic Review*, vol. 64, 3 June 1974.

Kumar, Arun, *The Black Economy in India*, with a new Foreword by V. P. Singh, New Delhi: Penguin Books India, 2002.

———'Curbing the Black Economy: Good Intentions Will Not Suffice', *Economic & Political Weekly*, 3 September 2016.

———'Estimation of the Size of the Black Economy in India, 1996-2012', *Economic & Political Weekly*, 26 November 2016.

———'High price, uncertain gain', *Indian Express*, 18 November 2016.

———'Demonetisation is a foolish step…The poor will suffer the most', interview with the author, *India Legal*, 24 November 2016.

———'Economic Consequences of Demonetisation: Money Supply and Economic Structure', *Economic & Political Weekly*, 7 January 2017.

———*Understanding the Black Economy and Black Money in India: An Enquiry into Causes, Consequences and Remedies*, New Delhi: Aleph Book Company, 2017.

Kurien, C. T., *The Market Economy: Theory, Ideology and Reality*, Founder's Day Lecture, Chennai: Madras Institute of Development Studies, 2015.

Lambsdorff, Johann Graf, 'Corruption and Rent-Seeking', *Public Choice* vol. 113.

Law Commission of India, Report No. 254 of the Law Commission of India, on The Prevention of Corruption (Amendment) Bill 2013, February 2015.

Mayadas, M., Lt. Gen. (retd.), *How the Bofors Affair Transformed India, 1989-1999*, New Delhi: Lancer Publishers, 1999.

Mayer, Robert, 'Marx, Lenin and the Corruption of the Working Class', *Political Studies*, XLI, 1993.

Mencher, Melvin, *News Reporting and Writing*, Eighth Edition, New

York: McGraw-Hill Higher Education, 2000.

Mukherjee, A. P., *Unknown Facets of Rajiv Gandhi, Jyoti Basu, Indrajit Gupta*, New Delhi: Manas Publications, 2014.

Murali, Kanta, *Caste, Class, and Capital: The Social and Political Origins of Economic Policy in India*, Cambridge: Cambridge University Press, 2017.

Myrdal, Gunnar, *Asian Drama: An Inquiry into the Poverty of Nations*, vols. 1, 2, and 3, New York: The Twentieth Century Fund, 1968.

——— 'The "Soft State" In Underdeveloped Countries', a chapter in *Unfashionable Economics: Essays In Honour of Lord Balogh* ed. Streeten, Paul, London: Weidenfeld and Nicolson, 1970.

Noorani, A. G., *Ministers' Misconduct*, New Delhi: Vikas Publishing House, 1973.

Obermayer, Bastian and Obermaier, Frederik, *The Panama Papers: Breaking the Story of How the Rich & Powerful Hide Their Money*, London: Oneworld Publications, 2016.

Oza, B. M., *Bofors: The Ambassador's Evidence*, New Delhi: Konark Publishers, 1997.

Pandian, M. S. S., *The Image Trap: M. G. Ramachandran in Film and Politics*, New Delhi: Sage Publications, 1992.

Patnaik, Prabhat, *Economics and Egalitarianism*, New Delhi: Oxford University Press, 1991.

Pattali Makkal Katchi (PMK), 'Subject: Corruption and misuse of power by the Ministers and Government of Tamil Nadu—request for calling a report from the Chief Minister of Tamil Nadu—demand for constituting an Enquiry Commission', memorandum submitted to the Governor of Tamil Nadu, K. Rosaiah, 17 February 2015.

Pavarala, Vinod, *Interpreting Corruption: Elite Perspectives in India*, New Delhi: Sage Publications, 1996.

Philby, Kim, *My Silent War: The Soviet Master Agent Tells His Own Story*, New York: Grove Press, INC., 1968.

Press Council of India (2009), 'Sub-Committee Report on "Paid News": How corruption in the Indian media undermines democracy', 7 October 2009.

——— 'Report on Paid News', 30 July 2010.

——— 'Report of the Election Coverage Monitoring Committee on Paid News during Gujarat Election—2012', adopted by the Council on 18 February 2013.

Quah, Jon S. T., 'Curbing Corruption in India: An Impossible Dream?', *Asian Journal of Political Science*, vol. 16, 3, 2008.

Ram, N., 'An Independent Press and Anti-hunger Strategies: The Indian Experience', *The Political Economy of Hunger: Volume I: Entitlement and Well-being,* eds. Jean Dreze and Amartya Sen, Oxford: Clarendon Press, 1991.

————'The Great Indian Media Bazaar: Emerging Trends and Issues for the Future', *India: Another Millennium?* ed. Romila Thapar, New Delhi: Penguin Books, 2000.

————*The Changing Role of the News Media in Contemporary India*, address as president of the Contemporary India section of the Indian History Congress, 72nd Session, Patiala, 10 December 2011.

————*Sharing the Best and the Worst: The Indian News Media in a Global Context*, James Cameron Memorial Lecture, City University London, 3 October 2012.

Reddy, C. Rammanohar, *Demonetisation and Black Money*, with a Foreword by Y. V. Reddy, Hyderabad: Orient Black Swan, 2017.

Sagayam, U., Report (in Tamil), dated 5 May 2012, submitted by U. Sagayam, Madurai district Collector to the Principal Secretary, Industries Department, Government of Tamil Nadu, 2012.

————Probe into Granite Mining Activities in Madurai District: Report Submitted to the Hon'ble High Court Madras by Thiru U. Sagayam, I.A.S., Special Officer/Legal Commissioner, 23 November 2015, 624 pages.

Santhanam Committee, Report of The Committee on Prevention of Corruption, Ministry of Home Affairs, Government of India, New Delhi, 1964, digitized copy.

Sarkaria Commission of Inquiry, *Final Reports,* vols. 1, 2, 3 & 4, Madras: Government of Tamil Nadu, 1978.

Sen, Amartya, *On Economic Inequality*, New Delhi: Oxford University Press, 1975.

————'Beyond Liberalization: Social Opportunity and Human Capability', the First D. T. Lakdawala Memorial Lecture, New Delhi: Institute of Social Sciences, 1994.

————*The Country of First Boys*, eds. Antara Dev Sen and Pratik Kanjilal, New Delhi: Oxford University Press, 2015.

Shakespeare, William (1599), *Julius Caesar* (1599), *The Oxford Shakespeare: The Complete Works*, second edition, Oxford: Clarendon Press, 2005.

Shankar, Shylashri & Gaija, Raghav, *Battling Corruption: Has NREGA Reached India's Rural Poor?*, New Delhi: Oxford University Press, 2013.

Singh, Joginder, *Inside CBI*, New Delhi: Chandrika Publications, 1999.

Sukhtankar, Sandip and Vaishnav, Milan, 'Corruption in India: Bridging Research Evidence and Policy Options', paper presented at the India Policy Forum, 2015.

Supreme Court of India, judgment of two-member bench comprising Justices Pinaki Chandra Ghose and Amitava Roy in 'Criminal Appeal Nos 300-303 of 2017, State of Karnataka, appellants vs Selvi J. Jayalalithaa & ors, respondents', etc.

Swaminathan, Madhura, 'Dangers of narrow targeting', *Frontline*, 31 October 1997.

———*Weakening Welfare*, New Delhi: Left Word Books, 2000.

———'Errors of Targeting: Public Distribution of Food in a Maharashtra Village, 1995-2000', *Economic and Political Weekly*, 6 July 2001.

———'Targeted food stamps', *The Hindu*, 3 August 2004.

———'Public distribution system and social exclusion', *The Hindu*, 7 May 2008.

———'Programmes to Protect the Hungry: Lessons from India', working paper for the United Nations Department of Economic and Social Affairs, New York, October 2008.

Tulloch, Gordon, 'The Welfare Costs of Tariffs, Monopolies, and Theft', *Western Economic Journal*, 5:3, June 1967.

United Nations Convention Against Corruption, adopted by the UN General Assembly on October 31, 2003 by resolution 58/4, and entered into force on December 14, 2005, New York: United Nations, 2004.

Viswanathan, Shiv, 'The Necessity of Corruption', *Seminar*, October 2008.

Vaishnav, Milan, *When Crime Pays: Money and Muscle in Indian Politics*, New Delhi: HarperCollins Publishers India, 2017.

Vittal, N., *Ending Corruption? How to Clean Up India*, New Delhi: Penguin Books, 2012.

Wade, Robert, 'The system of administrative and political corruption: Canal irrigation in South India', *The Journal of Development Studies*, vol. 18, 3, 1982.

Westander, Henrik, *Classified: The Political Cover-up of the Bofors Scandal*, trans. Saam Kapadia from the Swedish original, Bombay: Sterling Newspapers, 1992.

Williams, Martin, *Parliament Ltd: A Journey to the Dark Heart of British Politics*, London: Hodder & Stoughton, 2016.

Wyatt, Andrew, 'Populism and Politics in Contemporary Tamil Nadu', *Contemporary South Asia*, vol. 21, no. 4, 2013.

——— 'Combining Clientelist and Programmatic Politics in Tamil Nadu, South India', *Commonwealth & Comparative Politics*, vol. 51, no. 1, 2013.

INDEX

Adarsh Housing Society
  scandal, 12
Algernon, Carl-Fredrik, 88
Anna Dravida Munnetra
  Kazhagam (ADMK), 123
Annadurai, C. N., 122
Annan, General Kofi A., 68
anti-corruption campaigns,
  9–11, 23, 32–33, 34,
  137–139
anti-corruption law, 32–35
  enforcement of, 42–45
  Lokpal and Lokayuktas Act
    2013, 39–41, 138
  whistleblower protection
    law, 36–39, 139
Antrix Devas/ISRO Spectrum
  Allocation scandal, 12
Antulay case, 32
arms trade corruption, 16–17
*Asian Drama: An Inquiry into
  the Poverty of Nations,* 6
Asiatic corruption, 51–53
Associated Chambers of
  Commerce of India
  (ASSOCHAM), 18

Bardhan, Pranab, 7, 62, 76
Baskar, Dr C. Vijaya, 131
Basu, Debashis, 17
*Battling Corruption: Has
  NREGA Reached India's
  Rural Poor?,* 26
Baxi, Upendra, 7, 32, 33
Bhushan, Prashant, 60
black economy, xxvi
black money, 15
  relationship between
    corruption and, 16
Bofors scandal, xiii, xvi, xxiii–
  xxiv, xxiv, 83–105
  background, 84–86, 94–98

cover-up strategy, 100
damage limitation and cover-up efforts, 89
The Hindu's investigation, 90–94
transactions involved, 87–88
Boston Globe's investigation and exposé of sexual abuse of children, xviii
Bratsis, Peter, 71
bureaucratic corruption, 24
Burke, Edmund, 4

Cameron, James, 3
Capital (Karl Marx), 73
Cash for Votes scandal of 2008, 12
Central Vigilance Commission (CVC), 33
Chandrasekhar, C. P., 78
Clive, Robert, 4
Coalgate scandal, 12
Cognizant Technology Solutions Corp., 59–60
Committee on Prevention of Corruption, 5
Commonwealth Games scam, 12
Commonwealth Human Rights Initiative (CHRI), 44–45
Companies Act 2013, 150
The Confidence-Man (Herman Melville), xv
Cornwallis, Lord, 4
corporate fraud, 17–19
corruption, conceptualization of, 62–63
economists' views, 63–66
political views, 66–69
corruption in India, 3–4, 50
in days of the East India Company, 4, 51–53
deregulation and liberalization, role of, 13–14
difficulty of defining, 5–6
measure of, 5
period 2000-2013, 12
ranking, 56
stock explanation, 13
supply side of corruption, 6

Dagens Eko news broadcast, 84–85
Dalal, Sucheta, 17
decentralization and corruption, 25–27
defence deal scams (Tatra Trucks and AgustaWestland Helicopters), 12
demonetization, xxv
disclosure of information, 37–38

Editors' Guild of India, 29
Election Commission of India, 29
Emergency of 1975-1977, xix, 7

A Feast of Vultures (Josy Joseph), 58
Finance Act 2017, 149, 150, 151
folklore of corruption, 7, 9, 56
Foodgrains scandal, 12

Gandhi, Mahatma, 50
Gandhi, Rajiv, 21–23, 33, 84, 93, 94, 97–98
global data of corruption, 55
grand corruption scandal, xxii–xiv, 23
   Uttar Pradesh food grains scam, 24–25
2G Spectrum scam, 12
Gupta, Akhil, 8

Harshad Mehta security scam of 1992, 17–18
Hazare, Anna, 11, 39
Hinduja, G. P., 85

Income Tax Act 1961, 150
income tax raids, 130

investigative reporting, xix–xx, 99
   bribery of foreign officials, 59–60
   bribes and kickbacks as commissions, 58

Jayalalithaa case, 41, xxvii–xxviii
journalism, xvii–xviii, 156–162
   investigative, xix–xx
   laws restricting freedom of expression, xix

Kalyanasundaram, M., 123
Karat, Prakash, 72
Karunanidhi, M., 123
Kejriwal, Arvind, 39
Ketan Parekh stock market manipulation scam of 2001, 17–18
knowledgeable social actors, 8
Kroll Inc., 18

Law Commission, 34, 38–39
law enforcement, 60
licence raj, 13
localized corruption, 8
Lokpal and Lokayuktas Act 2013, 39–41, 138

Maharashtra Irrigation Scam, 12

Mahatma Gandhi National Rural Employment Guarantee Scheme, 120
Marxist understanding of political corruption, 70–79
  contemporary, 74–75
  deregulation and liberalization, 76–79
Menon, Krishna, 54
Modi, Narendra, xxv
money laundering, 15
Mukherjee, A. P., 21–23
Murali, Kanta, 77
Myrdal, Gunnar, 6–10

Narayan, Jayaprakash, 11
National Crime Record Bureau (NCRB), 44
National Rural Employment Guarantee Act (NREGA) scheme, 27
news media corruption, 27–31
Nigam, N. S., 40
Nilsson, Magnus, 84–85
Nobel Kemi AB arms scandals, 87–88

offence of criminal misconduct, 35–36
Official Secrets Act 1923, 37, 38

paid news, 27–30
Pandian, M. S. S., 125
petty corruption, 23–24
political corruption, xiii–xiv, 24
  cash donations to political parties, xxi–xxii, 21–23
  controversies over, 53–54
  immunity attaching to, 42
  against Jayalalithaa, xxvii–xxviii
  Marxist understanding of, 70–79
  political leaders involved in, xxix
Press Council of India (PCI), 28–29
Prevention of Corruption Act 1988, xxvii, 33, 137
Prevention of Corruption (Amendment) Bill 2013, 33, 137–138
prevention of corruption in India, 136–164
  developing capabilities to anticipate and prevent corruption, 153–156
  developing enforcement capacity, 139–140
  developing legislative actions, 137–139
  judicial accountability in

adjudicating corruption cases, 152–153
political education and mobilization, 162–164
raising the visibility of corporate and private sector fraud, 145–146
reforming and cleansing political finance and electoral funding, 146–152
role of journalism, 156–162
setting stricter, cleaner, and more effective regulation, 144–145
vigilance against grand corruption, 153–156
private sector fraud, 12, 17
PRS Legislative Research of the Prevention of Corruption (Amendment Bill) 2013, 35

Rajasekaran, Ilangovan, 113
Rajshekhar, M., 114
Ramachandran (MGR), M. G., 123, 125
Rao, P. Rama Mohana, 130
Ravishankar, Sandhya, 114
Reddy, J. Sekhar, 130
rent-seeking, 64
Representation of the People Act 1951, 150
Reserve Bank of India Act 1934, 150
Right to Information Act 2005 (RTI Act), 38
runaway electoral funding, 19–20

Sagayam, U., 115–119
Sahara India Pariwar Investor scam, 12, 18
Sainath, P., 27
Santhanam, K., 33
Saradha Group Chit Fund scam, 12, 18
Sarkaria, Ranjit Singh, 123–124
Satyam Computer Services mega-swindles, 12, 18
scam, etymology of, xv
Shah, A.P., 34
sharp practices, 30–31
Shourie, Arun, xix, 86
Singh, Charan, 25–26
Singh, Vishwanath Pratap, xxiii, 86
social formation, 73
South Asian countries, corruption in, 6–7, 9–10
Spotlight (film), xviii
Sreenivasulu, K., 130
State Industries Promotion

Corporation of Tamilnadu Limited (SIPCOT), 112
Statement of Objects and Reasons of the 2015 Amendment Bill, 34–35, 38

Taj Heritage Corridor scam, 12
Tamil Nadu's grand corruption system, xxvii–xxviii, 111–132
  beach sand mining operations, 113–115
  granite scam, 115–119
  involving TASMAC, 111–112, 125–127
  'populist' or welfare schemes, 120–122
  state's universal public distribution system, 112
Tamil Nadu State Marketing Corporation Limited (TASMAC), 125–127
Telgi Stamp scam, 12, 18
Transparency International (TI), xiii, 23, 56
  Bribe Payers Index, 57–58

Corruption Perception Index (CPI), 55

United Nations Convention Against Corruption (UNCAC), 67–69
United Progressive Alliance (UPA), 14
US Foreign Corrupt Practices Act (FCPA), 59
Uttar Pradesh food grains scam, 24–25
Uttar Pradesh National Rural Health Mission scam, 12

Verma, Alok Kumar, 61
Vyapam scam, 13, 106–109

Watergate investigation, xx
Whistleblowers Protection Act 2011, 36
Whistleblowers Protection (Amendment) Bill 2015, 37
Whistleblowers Protection Bill, 36

Xi Jinping, 79